little
GIANTS
number
puzzles
3+2+5=10
OVER 300 FUN
BRAINTEASERS

GW00632170

little
GIANTS
number
puzzles
3+2+5=10
OVER 300 FUN
BRAINTEASERS

Capella

This edition published in 2007 by Arcturus Publishing Limited
26/27 Bickels Yard, 151–153 Bermondsey Street,
London SE1 3HA

In Canada published for Indigo Books
468 King St W,
Suite 500,
Toronto,
Ontario M5V 1L8

ISBN-13: 978-1-84193-571-3

Illustrations & Page Layout by CREATIVE QUOTIENT

Printed in China

Contents

Over 300 fun brainteasers.

Think you don't like math and number problems? Then think again! Full of questions and brainteasers, *Number Puzzles* will give you hours of enjoyment – and don't worry, we even provide the answers!

Also in this book – Sudoku! The number game from Japan which is the craze now sweeping the world.

It's a very simple game. You don't need to be good at maths to play or even be able to add up, subtract or multiply. In fact, if you can count up to nine, you can play.

All you need to do is place a number from 1-9 in each empty square so that every row, column and 3x3 box contains a number.

We've even provided some pages at the back for your workings.

LINES OF THOUGHT

Put your thinking caps on and work out which number is missing from each line of octagons. Use the first line as an example.

A	3	5	8	12	17	23
B	7	9	12	16	21	27
C	1	3	6	10	15	21
D	8	10	13	17	22	28
E	2	4	7	11	16	22
F	10	12	15	19	24	30

PYRAMID POINTERS

Which number goes on the top point of pyramid C?

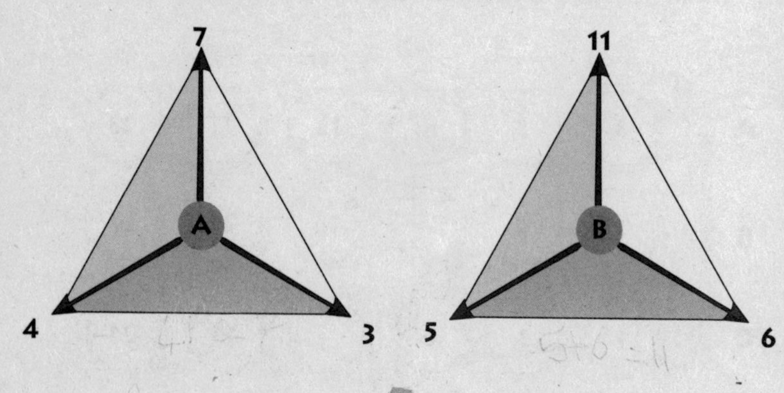

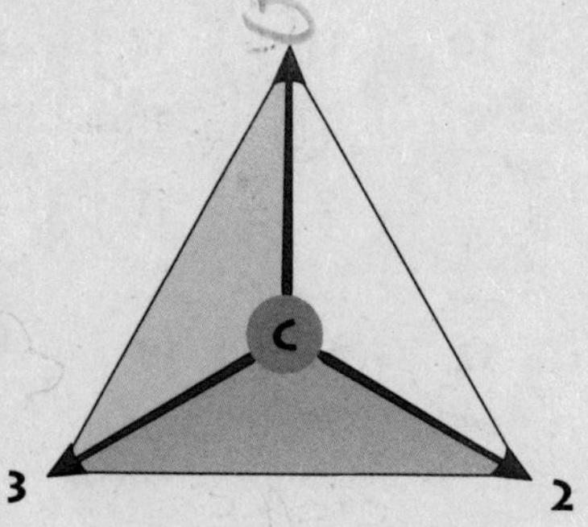

TIME OUT

What time should be shown on the blank watch at the end?

2 : 10

3 : 20

4 : 30

5 : 40

A: 7 : 10

B: 9 : 15

C: 6 : 50

D: 8 : 30

LEVEL 1

STAR STRUCK

Can you complete this puzzle by using the top two stars as a guide?

Star 1: 2, 4, 6, 8, 10

Star 2: 3, 6, 9, 12, 15

Star 3: 4, 8, ?, 16, 20

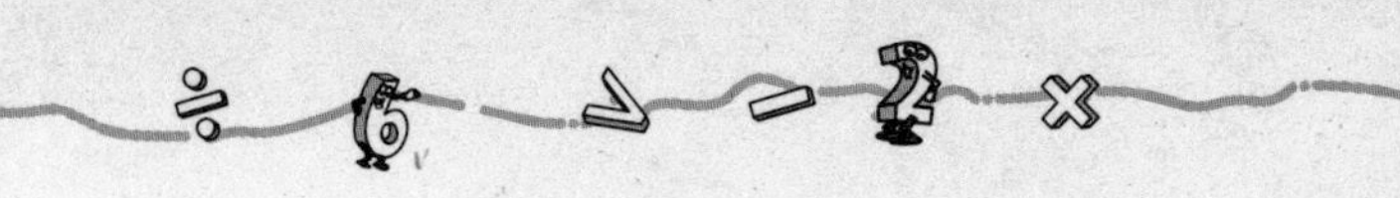

FIGURE-IT-OUT

Complete this puzzle by adding the correct number.
(Clue: Try looking at the puzzle from all directions.)

4	6	2
7	17	10
3	11	

SLICED UP!

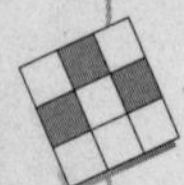

Can you work out which number is missing from the empty segment?
(Clue: Try cutting the circles in half.)

4 3 5
12 10 2

3 5 4
15 4

3 6 8
18 16 2

LEVEL 1

SUDOKU

1		8	5		7	6		4
	3		8	4	2	9	1	
4	2	7		6			3	8
8	1	4	7				6	9
6			3	9	4			5
9	5				8	7	4	2
7	4			5		8	9	3
	6	5	9	8	3		7	
3		9	4		1	2		6

LEVEL 1

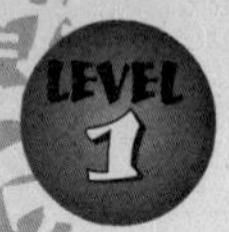

ODD ONE OUT

Which number is the odd one out in each wheel?

11
7
9
13
2
19
3
A
26
15
18
14
20
34
42
B

Because it's the only one that isn't a prime number.

Because it's the only odd number.

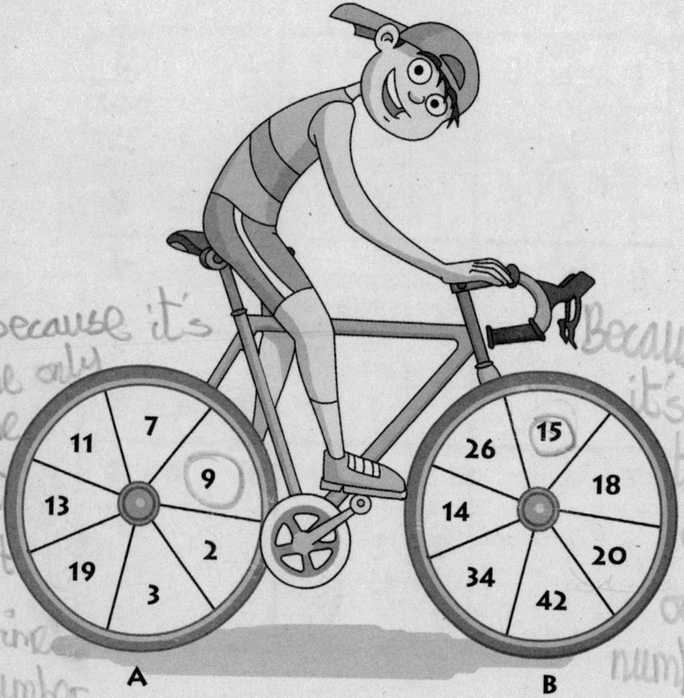

CRAZY CLOCKS

Look carefully at the sequence of clocks and fill in the blank.

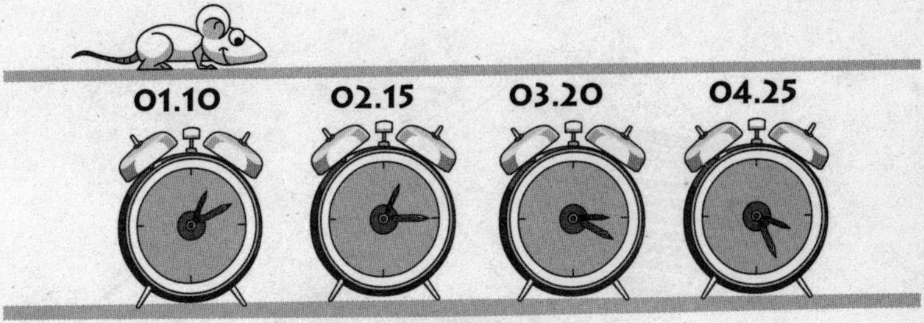

01.10 02.15 03.20 04.25

04.35 05.20 05.30 06.30

A B C D

PYRAMID POSER

Work out which number goes at the top of the third pyramid.

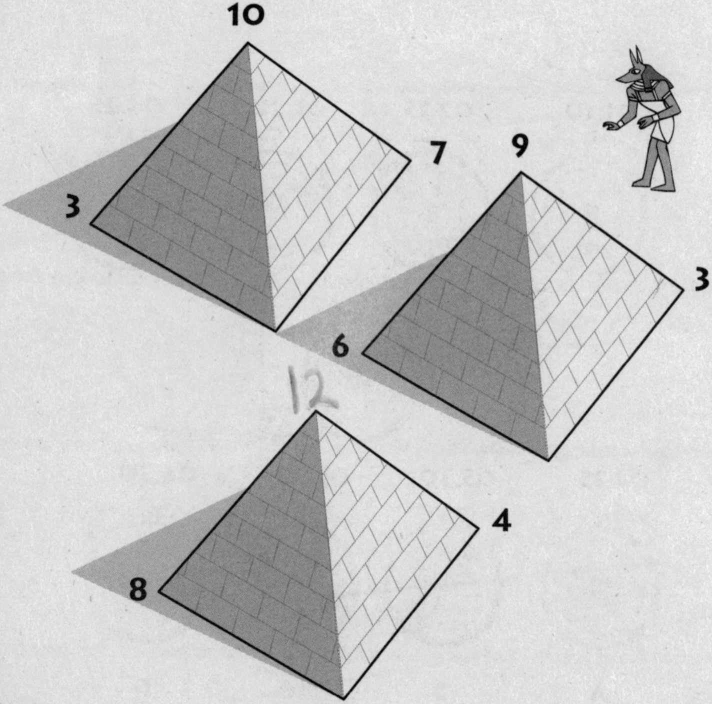

10

7

3

9

3

6

12

4

8

LEVEL 1

ALL SQUARE

Here is a complete puzzle - work out why it contains these numbers. (Clue: The centre square holds the answer.)

3	1	2	2
5	9	8	4
6	8	7	1
1	1	3	3

DOTTY DOMINOES!

Which of the six spare dominoes completes this dotty sequence?

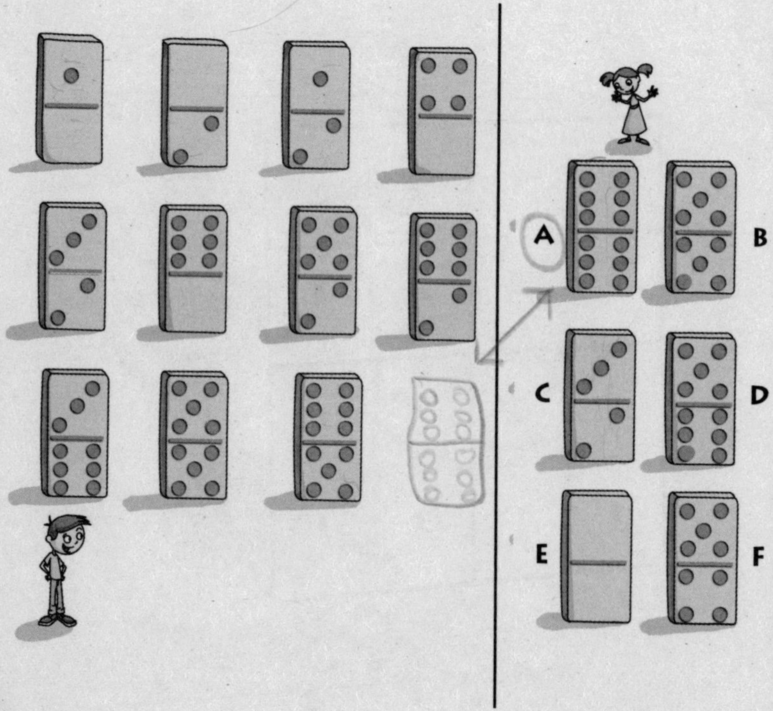

A

B

C

D

E

F

CIRCLES

Fill in the missing number.

SUDOKU

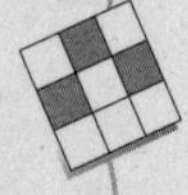

2	1	7	3	9	6	8	4	5
8	3	9	5	4	7	2	6	1
5	6	4	2	8	1	3	7	9
6	8	3	4	1	2	9	5	7
4	7	5	8	6	9	1	2	3
9	2	1	7	3	5	4	8	6
7	9	2	1	5	8	6	3	4
1	4	8	6	7	3	5	9	2
3	5	6	9	2	4	7	1	8

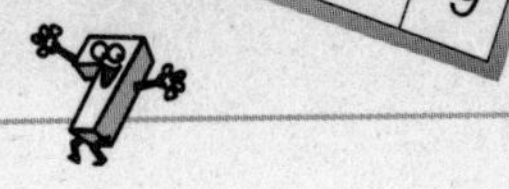

DIGITAL DISCS

Using the first two discs as an example, fill in the empty segment.

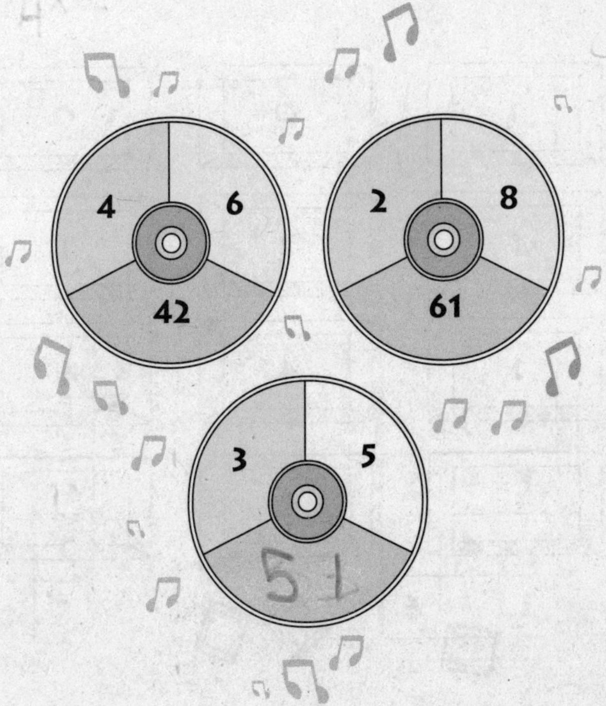

4 6 42

2 8 61

3 5

BOXING CLEVER

Can you work out which number is missing from the empty box?
(Clue: Think square numbers!)

CHOCOLATE 1	CHOCOLATE 0	CHOCOLATE 0
CHOCOLATE 1	CHOCOLATE 2	CHOCOLATE 1
CHOCOLATE 1	CHOCOLATE 4	CHOCOLATE 4
CHOCOLATE 1	CHOCOLATE 6	CHOCOLATE

FOUR SQUARE

Fill in the empty shape and complete the puzzle.
(Clue: Look carefully at the different shading to find the pattern.)

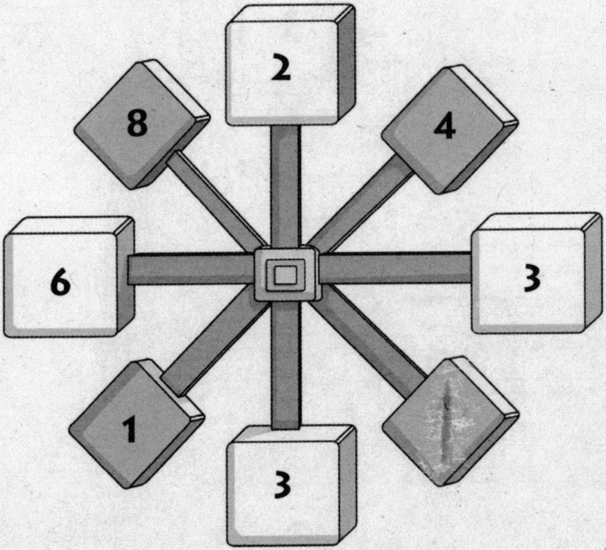

2

8 4

6 3

1

3

LEVEL 1

OUT OF PLACE

Which number doesn't go with the rest?

ET CETERA

Which number must be added to continue this sequence?

SUDOKU

1	6	4		2		8		
			7	8	6	4	1	
	8		4		1	9		6
2			3		5		7	
	3	5		6		1	9	
	7		2		9			4
6		2	5		8		4	
	5	7	6	3	4			
		8		9		7	6	5

LEVEL 1

DOMINOES

By counting the dots on these dominoes, can you work out which of the six spare pieces completes the sequence?

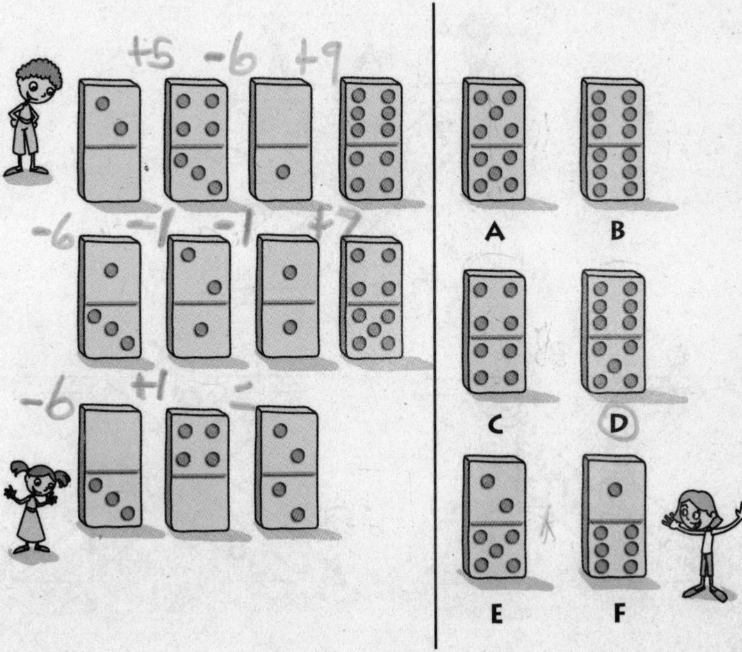

A

B

C

D

E

F

CROSS OVER

Which number is missing from each puzzle?

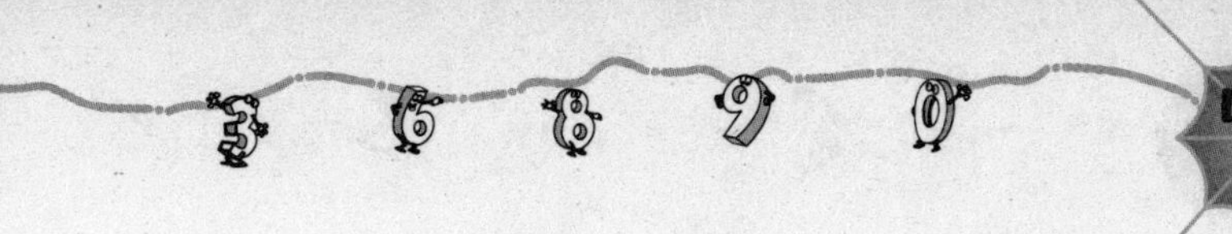

TRI - PIE

Which number is missing from the empty segment?
(Clue: Look at the matching segments on each circle.)

NUMBER BOX

Complete this number box by adding the correct number.
(Clue: The puzzle works up and down as well as side to side!)

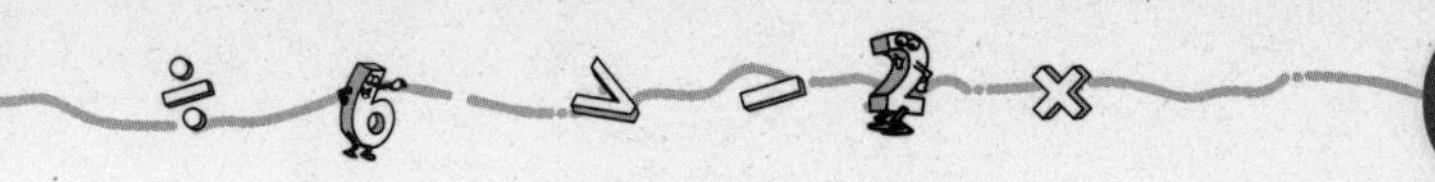

WEB WORLD

Which number replaces the question mark and completes the web? (Clue: Try rotating part of the web.)

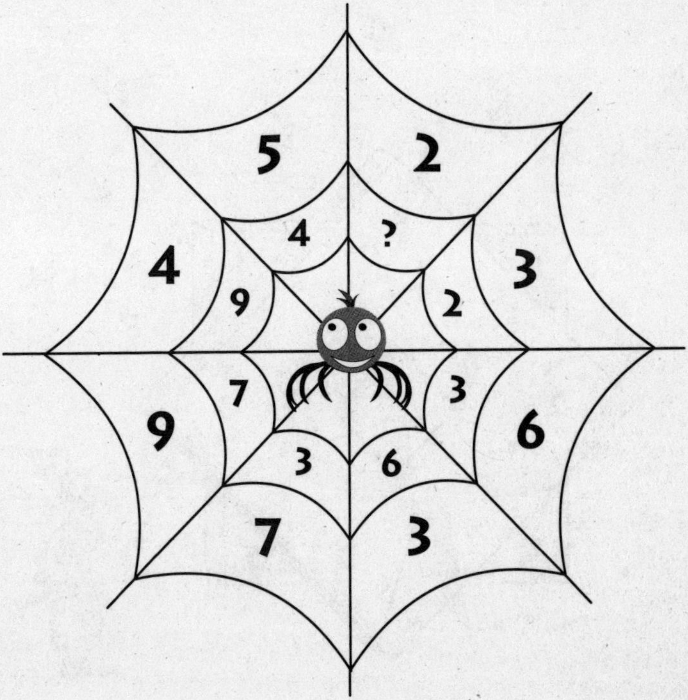

5 2

4 ?

4 3

9 2

7 3

9 6

3 6

7 3

MAGIC SQUARE

Fill in the empty space and complete the puzzle.
(Clue: Look carefully at the grid to find the pattern.)

4

8 1

2 3

1 5

6

ALL STAR

By using the first two stars as a guide, can you complete this puzzle?

3
21 6
9 15

2
6 4
20 12

45 10
20 35

CIRCLES

Which number is needed to finish the puzzle?

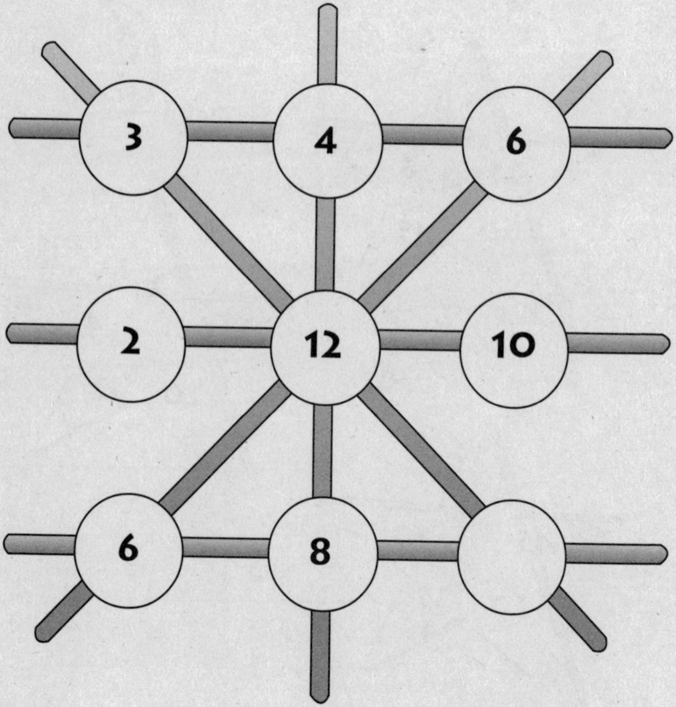

3	4	6
2	12	10
6	8	

1			7		8	2	5	
9	3		6				4	7
	7			4	3	8		
7	4	9	5	1				
8	2		4		7		6	5
				8	9	4	7	1
		6	3	5			2	
3	9				2		1	4
	1	5	9		4			8

NUMBER WHEEL

Replace the question mark in this wheel with the correct number. (Clue: Look at the numbers in opposite segments.)

SEQUENTIAL

Which number will complete this sequence?

LEVEL 1

HOLE IN ONE

We have left a hole in this puzzle. Can you fill it with the correct number? (Clue: Don't think in straight lines.)

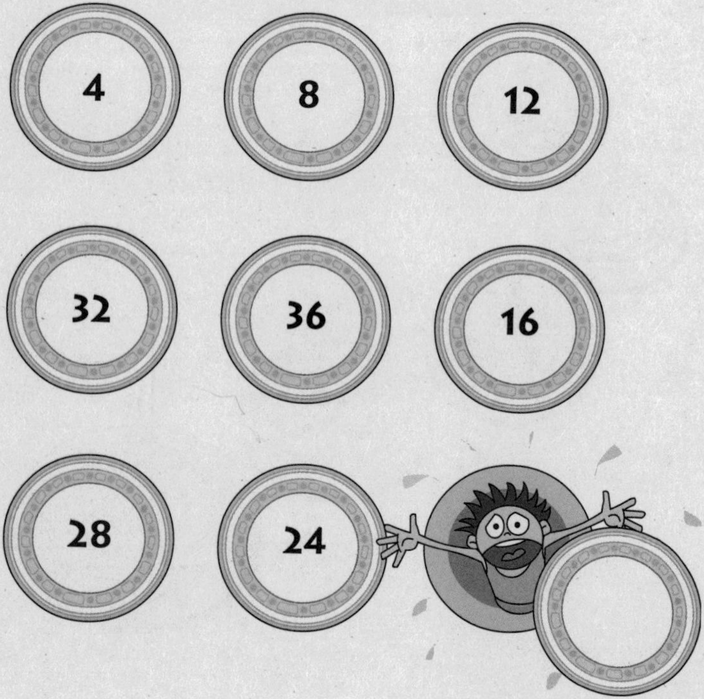

4	8	12
32	36	16
28	24	

MAGIC SQUARE

By using every number between 2 and 10 can you complete this number square so that every line, up and down, left to right and diagonal adds up to 18?

MISFITS

One number in each kite is a misfit, in other words it doesn't follow the same rules or requirements as all the others. Can you work out which one it is?

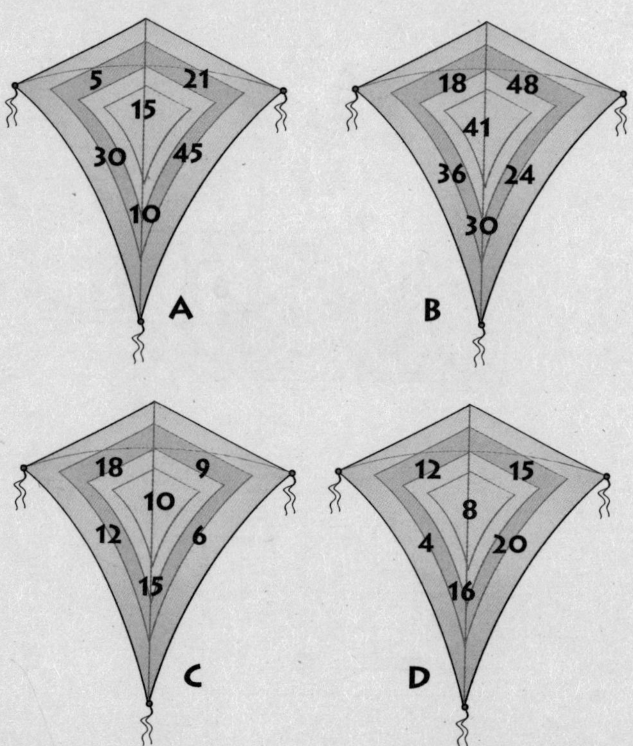

LEVEL 1

HOUSEY HOUSEY!

Using the first two houses as an example, can you work out which number is missing from the third house?

12

1 2

4 2 3

17

1 3

6 5 2

2 1

7 5 1

OPTIONAL EXTRAS

Which of the three optional extra numbers at the bottom will replace the question mark?
(Clue: Don't just look from left to right.)

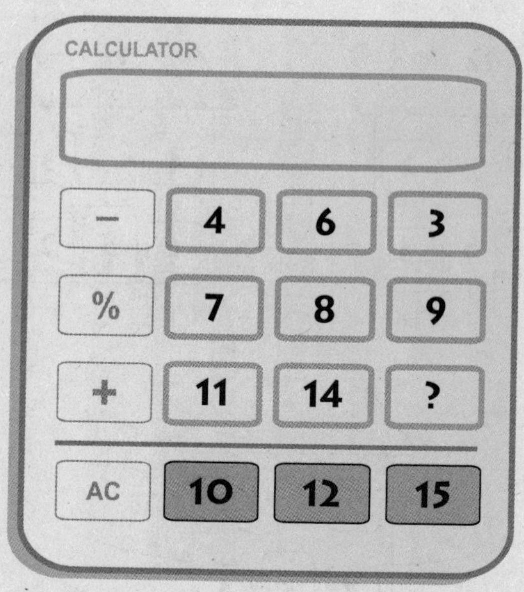

BOXING CLEVER

Which number completes this sequence?

2 3 5 9

MISSING NUMBERS

Which numbers are missing from the empty petals?
(Clue: Look at the matching segments,
the middle flower is the link!)

SUDOKU

1	3	5				2	7	8
		9	3	7	2	5		
	6				8		3	
		7		5	4		8	
2	4		1		3		6	5
	5		6	8		9		
	1		9				4	
		6	8	4	1	3		
9	2	4				8	5	1

HONEYCOMB

Which number is the odd one out?

5

15

11

22

35

HOLE NUMBERS

Complete this puzzle by adding the correct number to the empty circle. (Clue: Straight thinking will not help you with this one!)

FIGURE - IT - OUT

Which three-figure answer is missing from the empty box?

SHAPE UP

Find the missing number to complete the puzzle.

	3				4	
7		1		8		2
	5				6	
	7				6	
3		6		5		
	2				1	

LEVEL 1

TAKE AWAY

What number goes in the middle rectangle?
(Clue: It has got nothing to do with sums!)

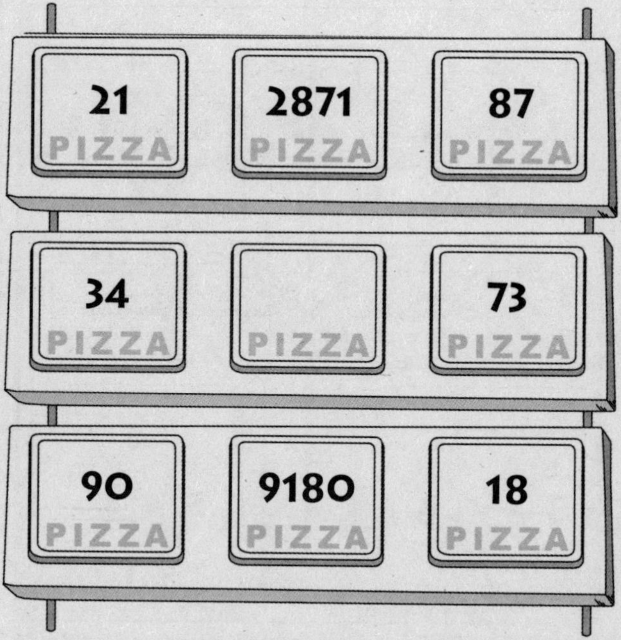

21 PIZZA	2871 PIZZA	87 PIZZA
34 PIZZA	PIZZA	73 PIZZA
90 PIZZA	9180 PIZZA	18 PIZZA

DOTTY!

Which of the bottom numbers will go into the centre dot?
(Clue: Look at both sides of the grid.)

5 4 1

2 7 1 8 2

1 3 4 ◯ 6 7 1

5 8 2 2 9

7 1 6

4 5 6 7

LEVEL 1

SUDOKU

<table>
<tr><td></td><td></td><td>3</td><td>1</td><td></td><td></td><td></td><td>9</td><td>6</td></tr>
<tr><td>6</td><td>1</td><td></td><td></td><td>9</td><td>2</td><td></td><td>3</td><td>5</td></tr>
<tr><td>8</td><td></td><td></td><td>6</td><td></td><td></td><td>7</td><td>2</td><td></td></tr>
<tr><td></td><td>8</td><td></td><td></td><td>5</td><td></td><td>3</td><td></td><td>2</td></tr>
<tr><td>7</td><td></td><td>5</td><td>2</td><td>4</td><td>6</td><td>1</td><td></td><td>9</td></tr>
<tr><td>4</td><td></td><td>9</td><td></td><td>1</td><td></td><td></td><td>6</td><td></td></tr>
<tr><td></td><td>6</td><td>1</td><td></td><td></td><td>3</td><td></td><td></td><td>4</td></tr>
<tr><td>3</td><td>4</td><td></td><td>9</td><td>7</td><td></td><td></td><td>5</td><td>8</td></tr>
<tr><td>9</td><td>7</td><td></td><td></td><td></td><td>4</td><td>2</td><td></td><td></td></tr>
</table>

NUMBER SQUARE

This puzzle is a little bit different in that we have given you all the numbers already to show you what the finished teaser looks like. Can you work out why these numbers are correct?

(Clue: The centre square is the key.)

2 5 3		7 1 2
	10	
6 3 1		6 2 2

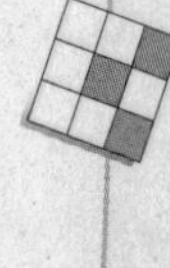

MINDBENDER

A stamp dealer bought a rare stamp for £70, sold it for £80, bought it back for £90 and sold it again for £100.
How much money did he make from all this trading?

To
Dear

from

NUMBER WINDOW

Work out which number should replace the question mark and complete the puzzle.

LEVEL 1

GONE MISSING!

The number in the middle column has gone missing. Can you replace it?

(Clue: Look at both sides of the grid.)

NETWORK

Complete this puzzle by finishing off grids A and B, using the first grid as an example.

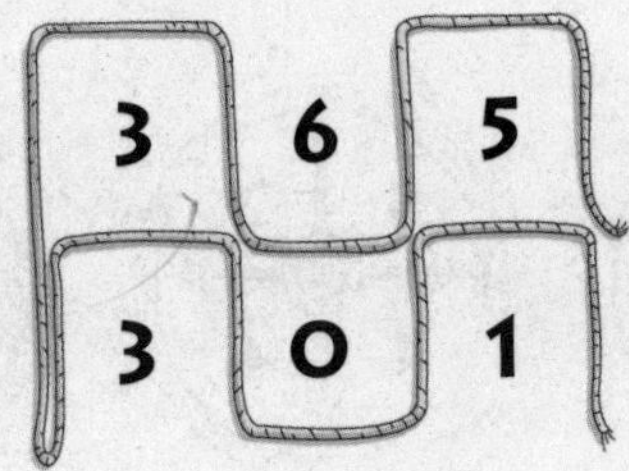

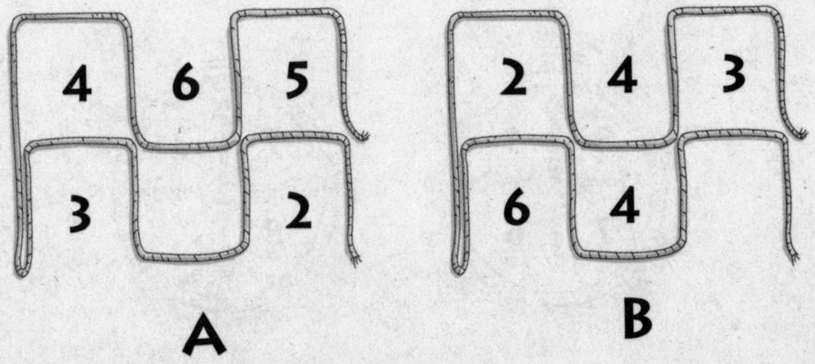

WHEEL SPIN

Which number is missing from the empty segment in the last wheel?
(Clue: The centre wheel in the top row is the link.)

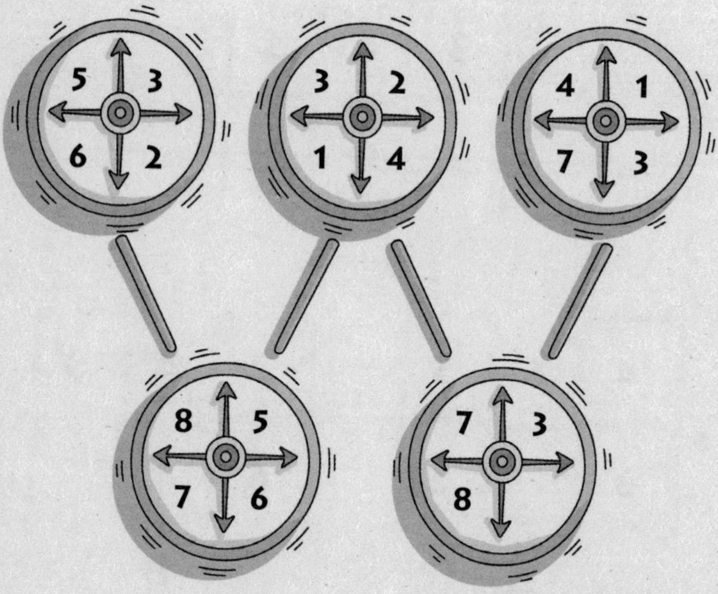

Wheel	Top left	Top right	Bottom left	Bottom right
Top row, left	5	3	6	2
Top row, centre	3	2	1	4
Top row, right	4	1	7	3
Bottom row, left	8	5	7	6
Bottom row, right	7	3	8	

SUDOKU

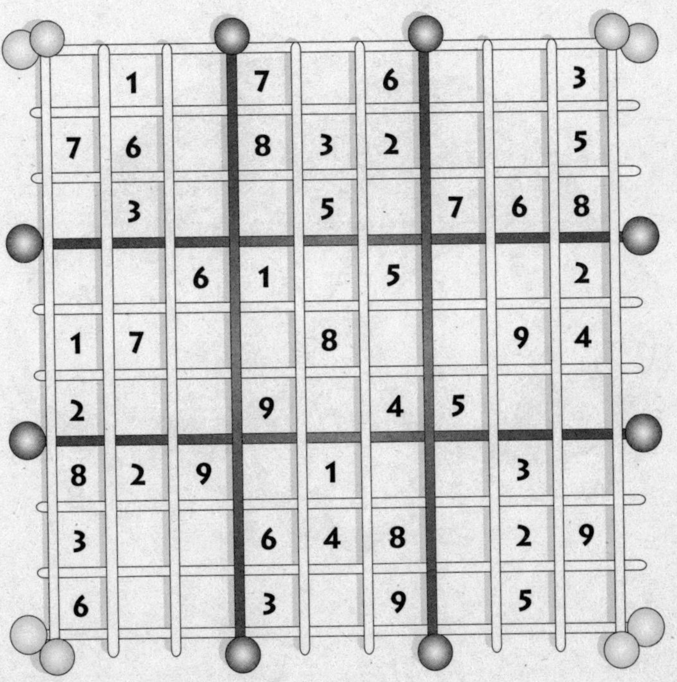

	1		7		6			3
7	6		8	3	2			5
	3			5		7	6	8
		6	1		5			2
1	7			8			9	4
2			9		4	5		
8	2	9		1			3	
3			6	4	8		2	9
6			3		9		5	

SPACE ODDITY

Look at this little boy's glasses very carefully and work out which number is the odd one out in each oval.

A

7
3 5
9 6
1

B

8
2 4
10 7
6

LEVEL 1

RING THE CHANGES

Which number goes in the empty ring?

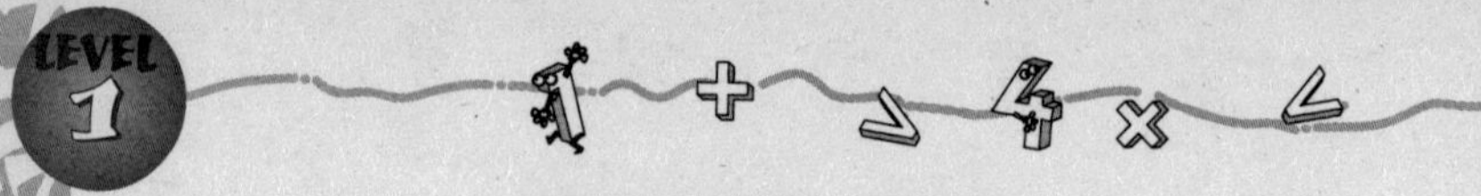

WHACKY WEB

Which number do you need to add in order to complete the web? (Clue: Try looking at opposite numbers.)

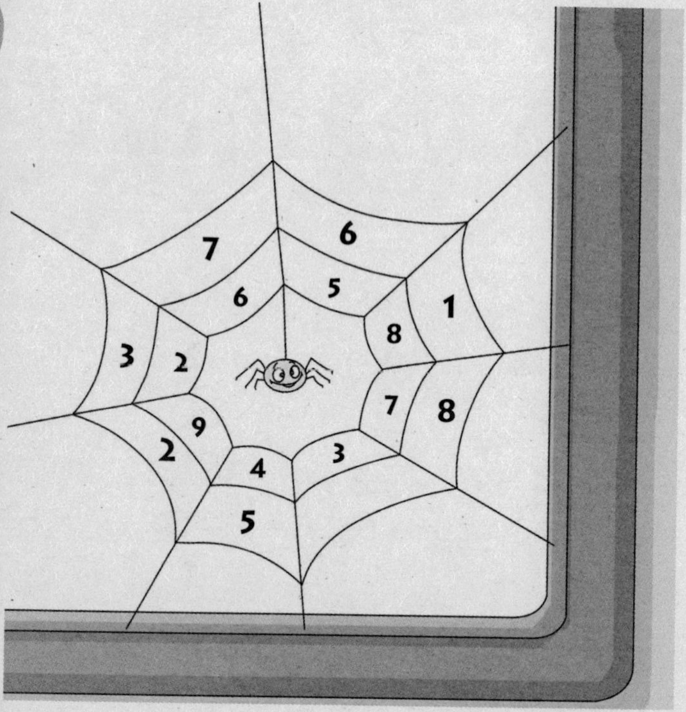

ROGUE NUMBER

In each book we have added a rogue number.
Can you work out which one it is?

A

11 14
16
8
4 18

B

13 10
22
20
18 6

C

12 7
15
3
21 9

D

11 5
13
16
23 25

MISSING LINK

Which number completes this chain?

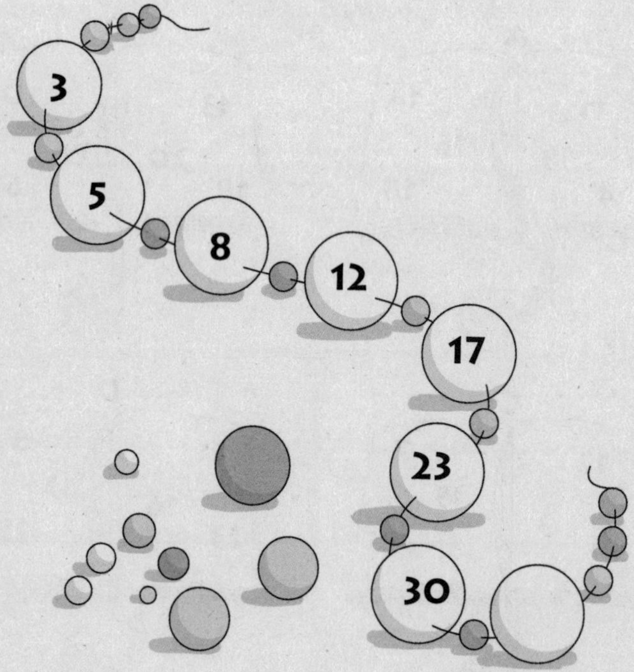

3

5

8

12

17

23

30

LINE UP

Using the same rule for every row, can you fill in the empty squares?

A	7	10	9	12	11	14
B	8	11	10		12	15
C	2		4	7	6	9
D	4	7		9	8	11
E	5	8	7	10		12
F	1	4	3	6	5	

LEVEL 1

CHANGE IT

Replace the question mark with the correct number.
(Clue: Look at the numbers within each segment.)

OPTIONS

Which of the three numbers at the bottom will complete this puzzle?

NUMBER SQUARE

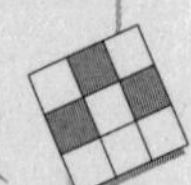

By using every number between 2 and 10 can you complete this number square so that every line, up and down, left to right and diagonal adds up to 18?

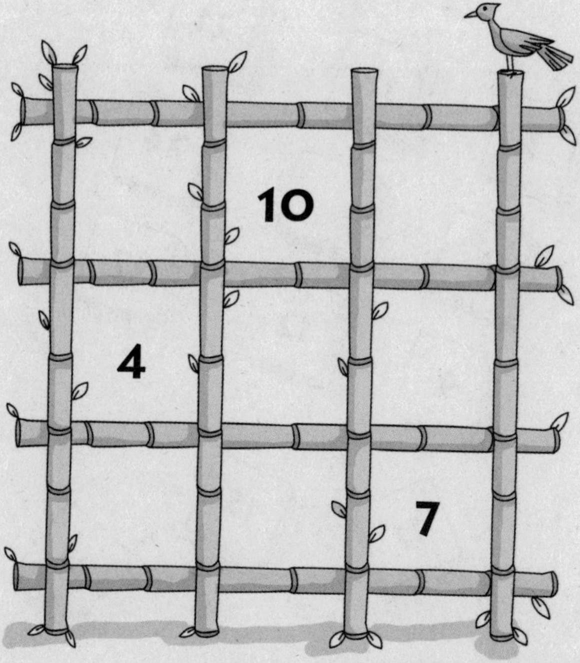

	10	
4		
		7

LEVEL 1

SUDOKU

9		1	4		3		7	
2			6	9		5		
	6				5	1	3	
				7	4	8	1	3
1		5		6		2		4
4	8	3	9	1				
	4	6	2				8	
		8		3	6			7
	1		8		7	9		5

STAR STRUCK

Using the two completed stars as an example, work out what missing number is in the third.

3
9 (10) 2
5 1

4
3
6 (11)
2
7

8
6 ( )
2 3
5

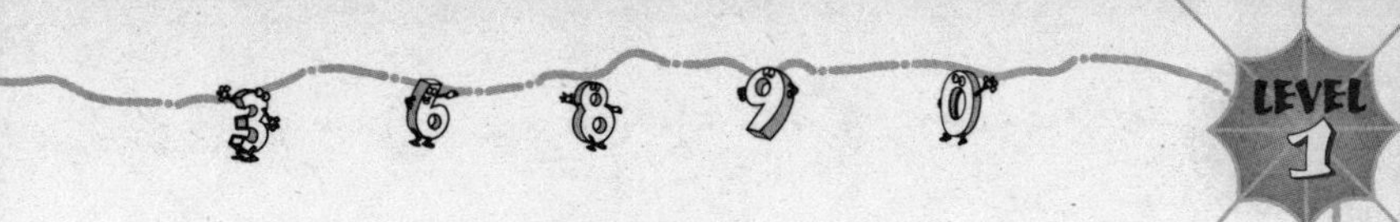

TRIO

Using the first two teddy bears as an example, fill in the empty space in the third.

4 3
24

7 2
28

3 8

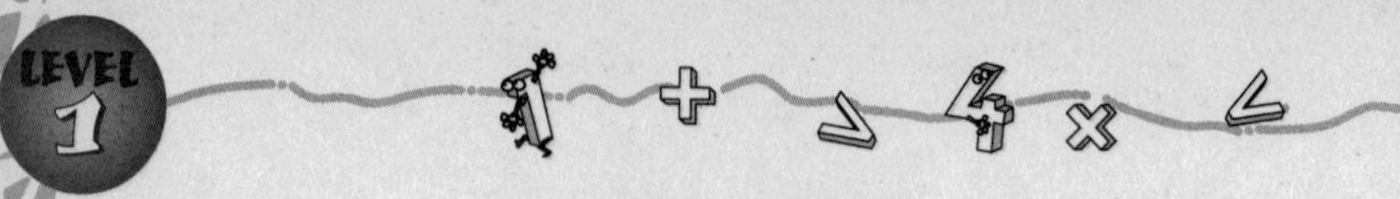

GRID LOCK

Can you work out which numbers are required to complete grids A & B?

6	4	7
1	3	0

2	8	5
7		4

A

3	0	8
5		0

B

LINES OF THOUGHT

Put your thinking cap on and work out which number is missing from each line of octagons. Use the first line as an example.

PYRAMID POINTERS

Which number goes on the top point of pyramid C?

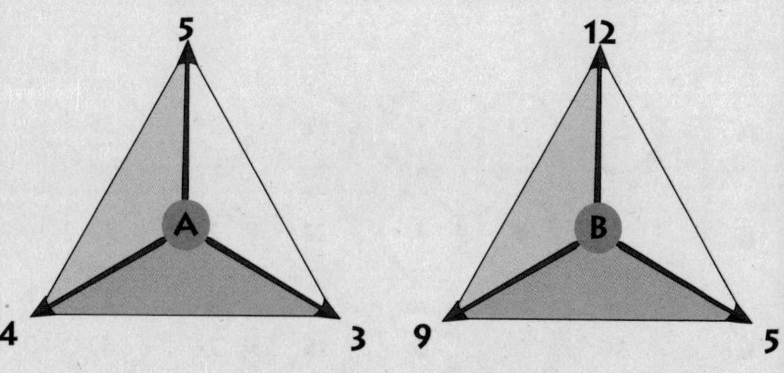

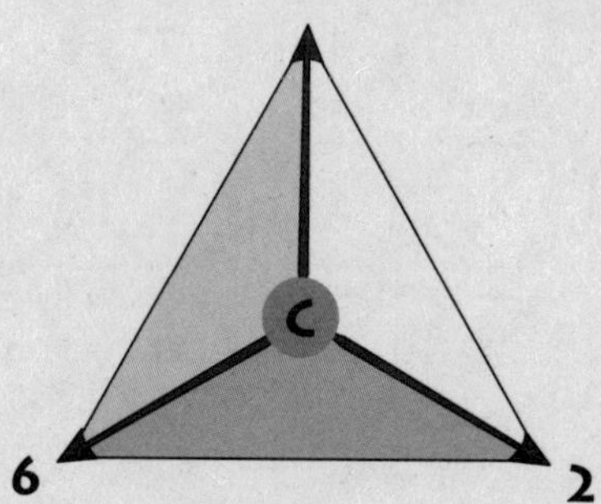

LEVEL 2

TIME OUT

What time should be shown on the blank watch at the end?

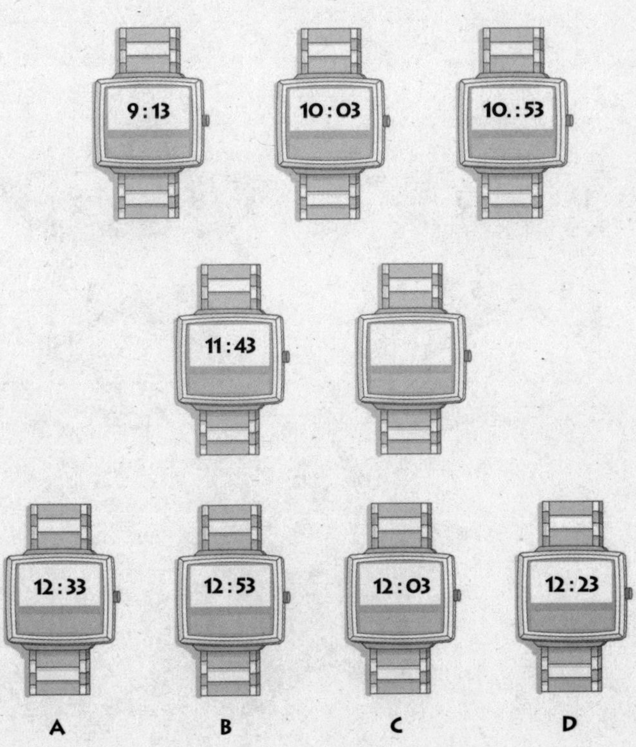

STAR STRUCK

Can you complete this puzzle by using the top two stars as a guide?

FIGURE-IT-OUT

Complete this puzzle by adding the correct number.
(Clue: Try looking at the puzzle from all directions.)

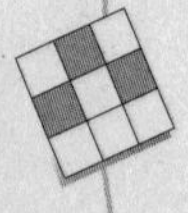

SUDOKU

		4	9			7		5
7	1	9		4	5		3	
2			8	3			4	
4	9			7		6		3
		1	2		3	8		
5		8		6			2	7
	6			2	4			1
	2		7	5		4	8	6
9		5			6	3		

LEVEL 2

SLICED UP!

Can you work out which number is missing from the empty segment? (Clue: Look at matching segments.)

LEVEL 2

DOTTY DOMINOES!

Which of the six spare dominoes completes this dotty sequence?

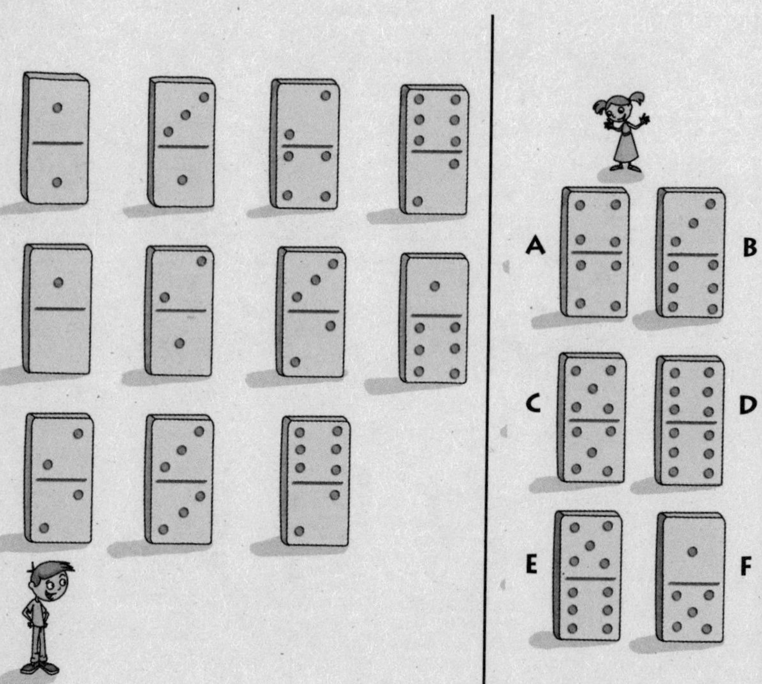

LEVEL 2

CIRCLES

Fill in the missing number.

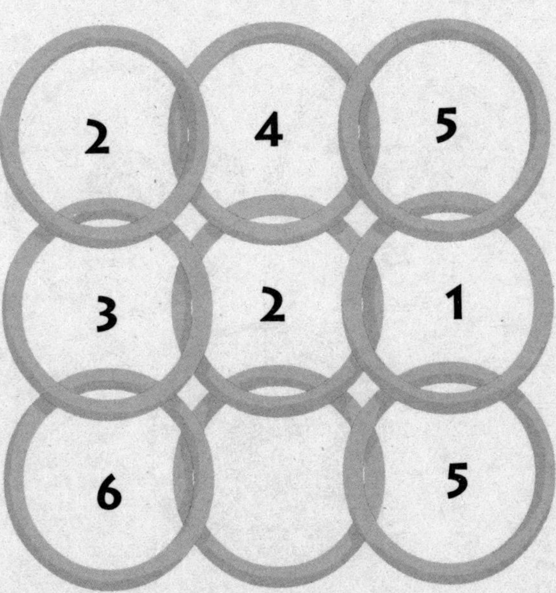

DIGITAL DISCS

Using the first two discs as an example, fill in the empty segment.

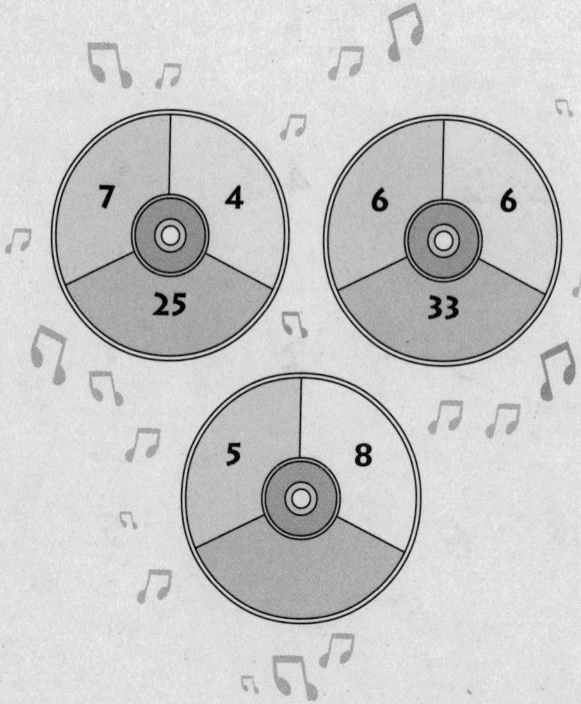

BOXING CLEVER

Can you work out which number is missing from the empty box?
(Clue: You might need a calculator for this one!)

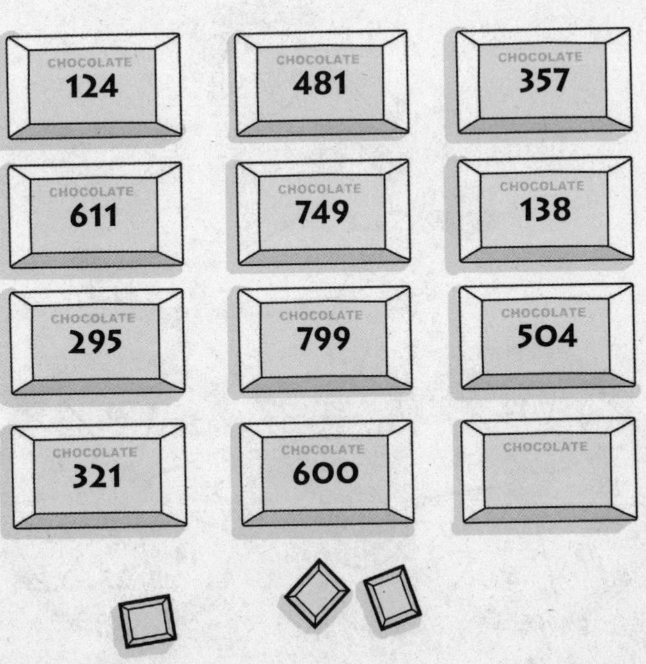

LEVEL 2

ODD ONE OUT

Which number is the odd one out in each wheel?

A: 9, 12, 3, 10, 6, 15, 18

B: 28, 21, 7, 42, 25, 14, 35

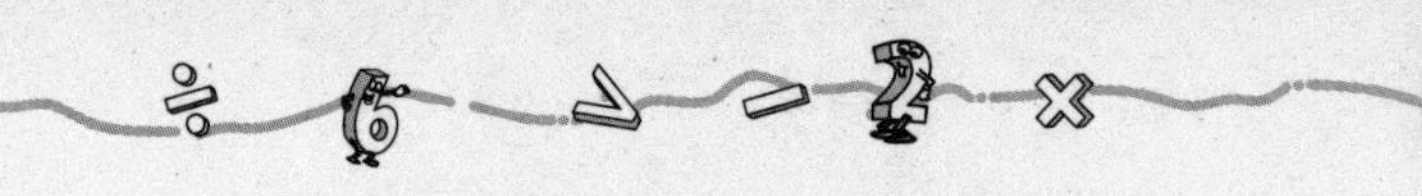

LEVEL 2

CRAZY CLOCKS

Look carefully at the sequence of clocks and fill in the blank.

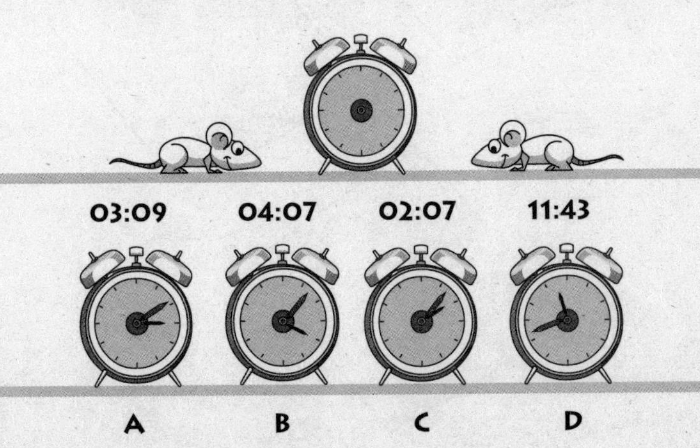

PYRAMID POSER

Work out which number goes at the top of the third pyramid.

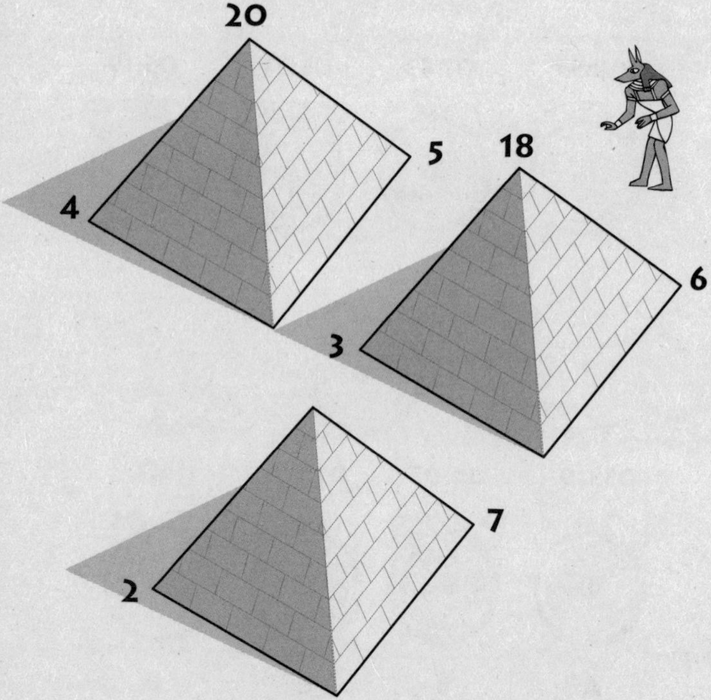

20

4 5

18

3 6

2 7

ALL SQUARE

Here is a complete puzzle - work out why it contains these numbers. (Clue: The centre square holds the answer.)

9	6	4	8
12	3	2	10
16	4	5	15
12	20	25	30

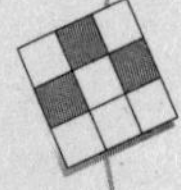

SUDOKU

9		6			8			
7	5			9			2	3
2			7	4		9		1
	7		2			3	4	8
	9		5	7	3		1	
3	6	2			4		7	
8		7		3	6			5
5	4			1			3	6
			9			4		7

DOMINOES

By counting the dots on these dominoes, can you work out which of the six spare pieces completes the sequence?

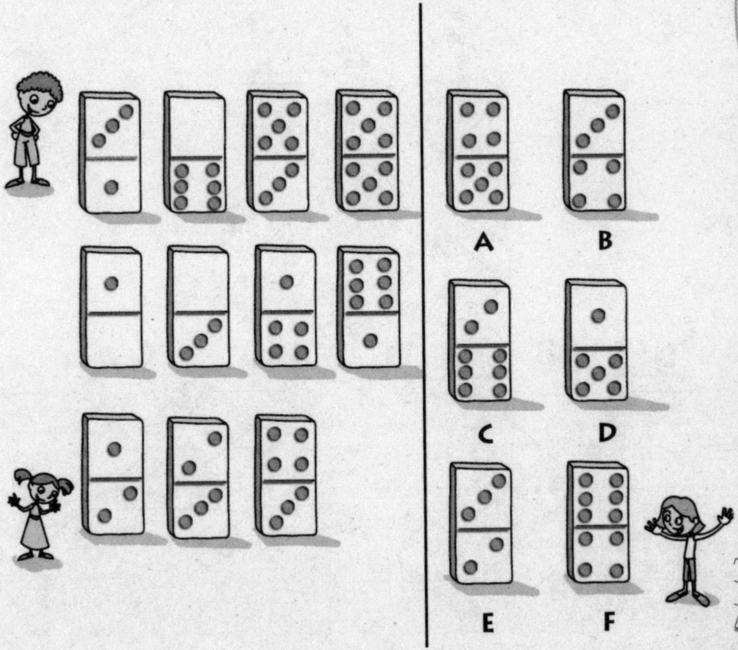

A B

C D

E F

CROSS OVER

Which number is missing from each puzzle?

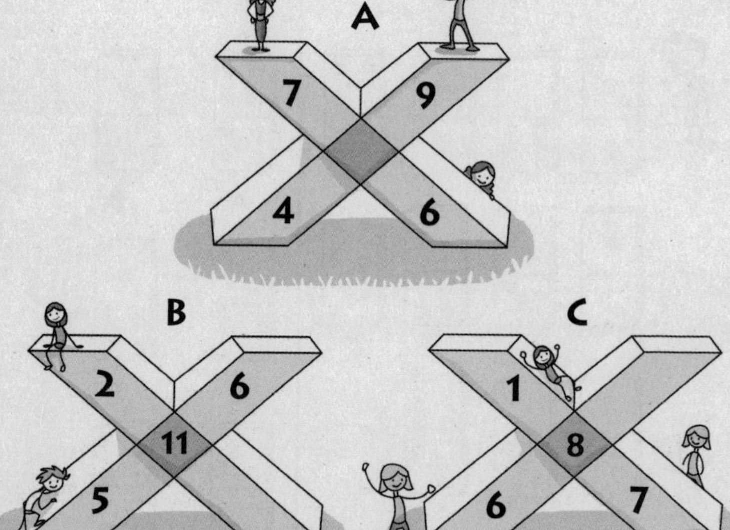

LEVEL 2

TRI - PIE

Which number is missing from the empty segment?
(Clue: Look at the matching segments on each circle.)

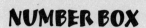

NUMBER BOX

Complete this number box by adding the correct number.
(Clue: The puzzle works up and down as well as side to side!)

BOXING CLEVER

Can you work out which number is missing from the empty box?
(Clue: You might need a calculator for this one!)

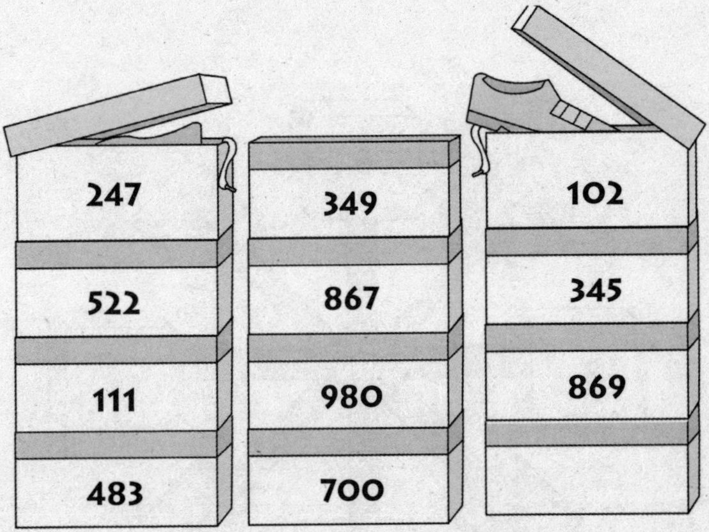

247	349	102
522	867	345
111	980	869
483	700	

LEVEL 2

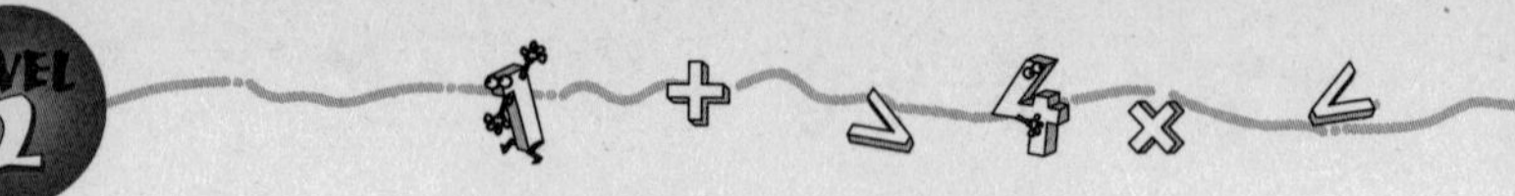

FOUR SQUARE

Fill in the empty shape and complete the puzzle.
(Clue: Look carefully at the different shading to find the pattern.)

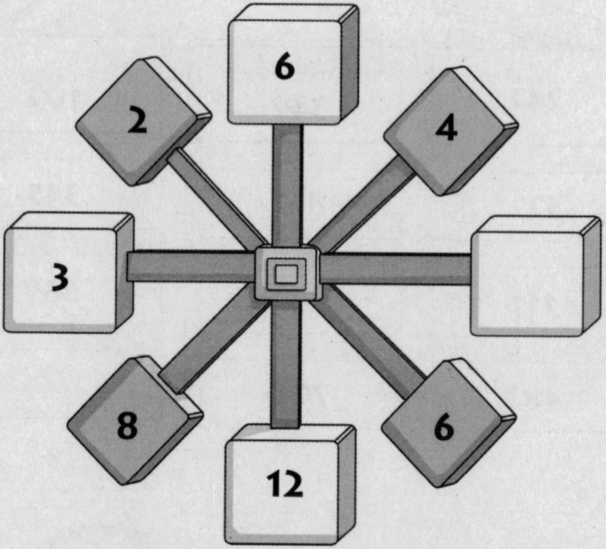

6

2 4

3

8 6

12

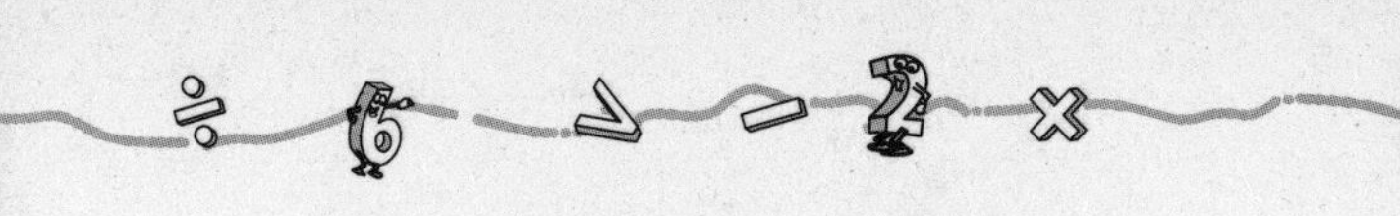

LEVEL 2

OUT OF PLACE

Which number doesn't go with the rest?

16

25

36

44

64

ET CETERA

Which number must be added to continue this sequence?

2 4 7 12 20 33 54

LEVEL 2

WEB WORLD

Which number replaces the question mark and completes the web?

(Clue: Try rotating part of the web.)

LEVEL 2

MAGIC SQUARE

Fill in the empty space and complete the puzzle.
(Clue: Look carefully at the grid to find the pattern.)

ALL STAR

By using the first two stars as a guide, can you complete this puzzle?
(Clue: Move from point to point.)

RING THE CHANGES

Which number goes in the empty ring?

SUDOKU

		3		9	6	7		
9	5	6		2		3	1	8
8					5			2
6		7	2					3
	3		1	7	8		6	
5					4	9		7
4			7					1
3	1	5		8		4	7	6
		8	5	4		2		

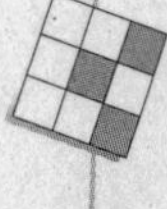

LEVEL 2

NUMBER WHEEL

Replace the question mark in this wheel with the correct number. (Clue: Look at the numbers in each segment as a group.)

SEQUENTIAL

Which number will complete this sequence?

LEVEL 2

HOLE IN ONE

We have left a hole in this puzzle. Can you fill it with the correct number? (Clue: Don't think in straight lines.)

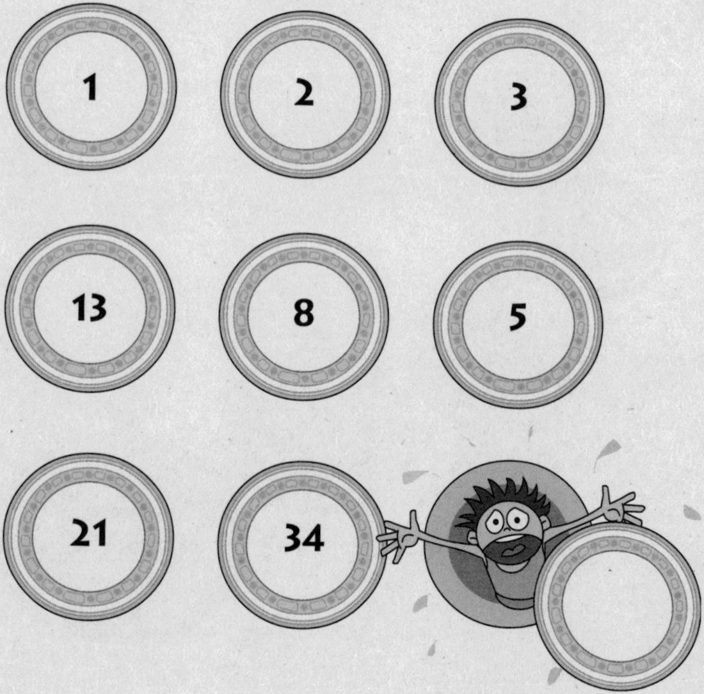

1	2	3
13	8	5
21	34	

MAGIC SQUARE

By using every number between 1 and 16 can you complete this number square so that every line, up and down, left to right and diagonal adds up to 34?

MISFITS

One number in each kite is a misfit, in other words it doesn't follow the same rules or requirements as all the others. Can you work out which one it is?

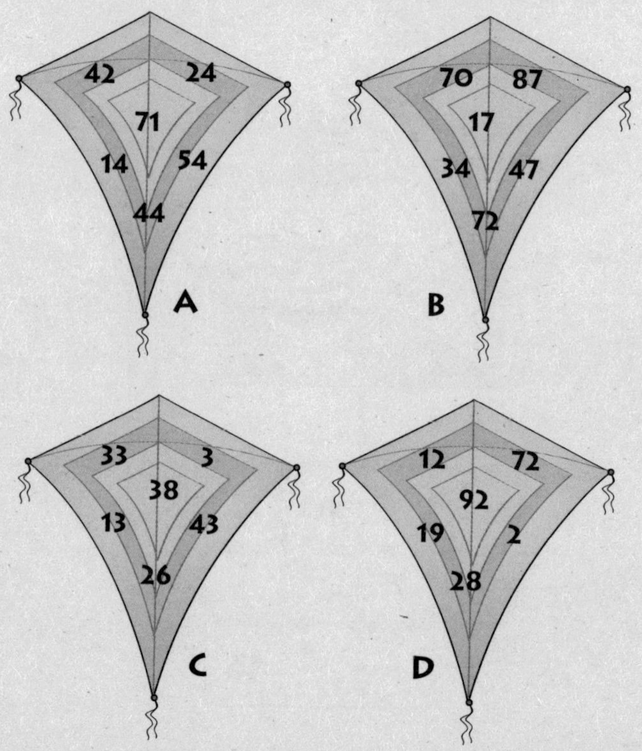

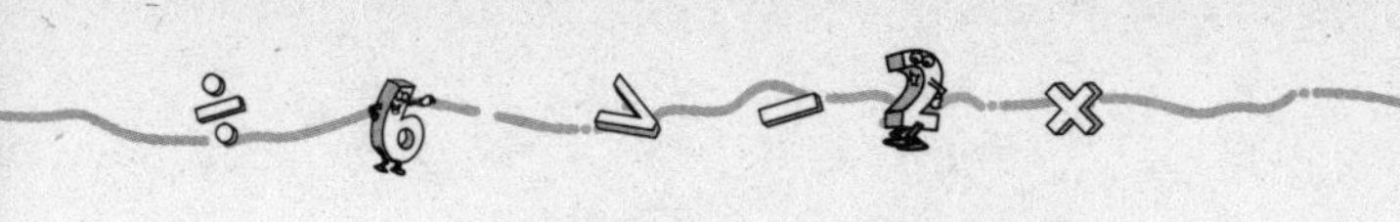

BOXING CLEVER

Which number completes this sequence?

2 4 10 28

MISSING NUMBERS

Which numbers are missing from the empty petals?
(Clue: Look at the matching segments, the middle flower is the link!)

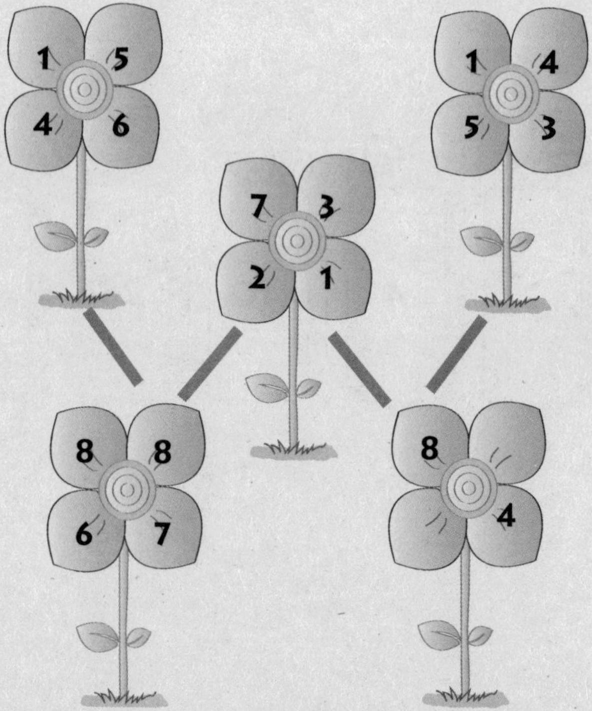

1 5
4 6

1 4
5 3

7 3
2 1

8 8
6 7

8
4

HONEY COMB

Which number is the odd one out?

4

18

12

23

28

HOLE NUMBERS

Complete this puzzle by adding the correct number to the empty circle.
(Clue: Straight thinking will not help you with this one!)

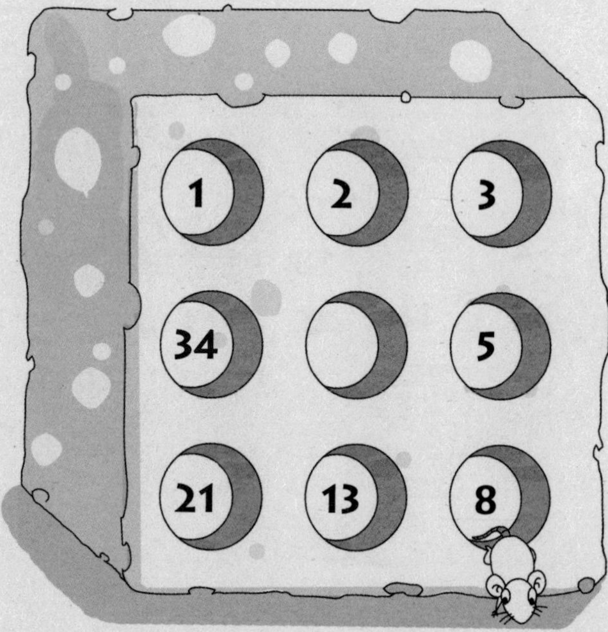

1	2	3
34		5
21	13	8

SUDOKU

	6	7		5	1			
3		5	9		8		1	
	8		6		7	2	4	
4				6	5			8
6	5			9			2	3
1			2	8				6
	2	4	5		6		9	
	9		3		2	7		4
			8	4		5	6	

LEVEL 2

FIGURE-IT-OUT

Which three-figure answer is missing from the empty box?

SHAPE UP

Find the missing number to complete the puzzle.

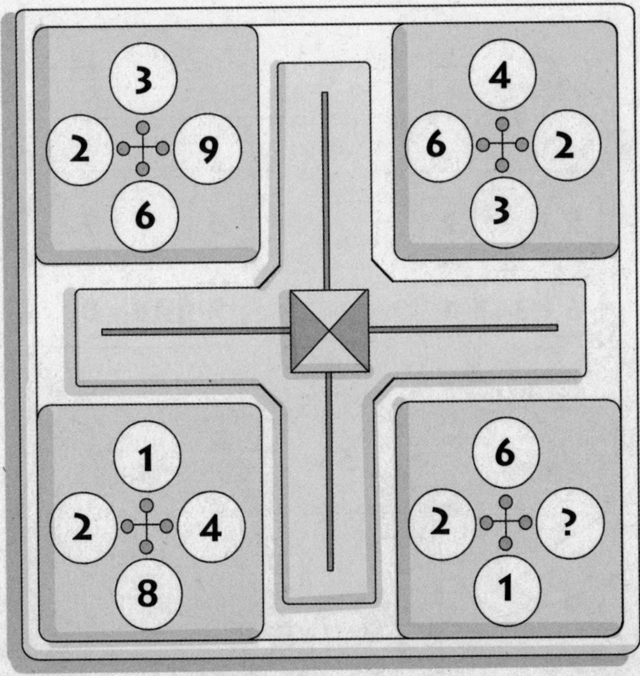

LEVEL 2

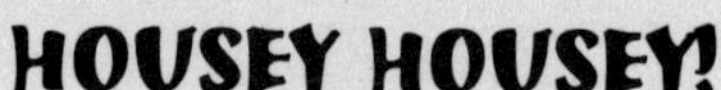

HOUSEY HOUSEY!

Using the first two houses as an example, can you work out which number is missing from the third house?

3

5 2

6 34 1

1

5 7

2 46 8

5

2 9

1 4

OPTIONAL EXTRAS

Which of the three optional extra numbers at the bottom will replace the question mark?
(Clue: Don't just look from left to right.)

CALCULATOR

–	2	22	29
%	4	16	37
+	7	11	?
AC	19	27	46

LEVEL 2

NUMBER SQUARE

This puzzle is a little bit different in that we have given you all the numbers already to show you what the finished teaser looks like. Can you work out why these numbers are correct?

(Clue: The centre square is the key.)

Top left		Top right	
4	3	8	1
3			4

Centre	
5	2
3	9

Bottom left		Bottom right	
3			4
2	7	1	1

MINDBENDER

Jack and Martha have been married for 20 years. If you add Jack's age to Martha's, you get a combined age of 91 years. Jack is now twice as old as Martha was when he was as old as she is now. From this information, can you work out how old Jack and Martha are now?

NUMBER WINDOW

Work out which number is missing and complete the puzzle.

3	2	7	3
1	4	2	3
4	9	11	4
7	5	3	

GONE MISSING!

The number in the middle column has gone missing.
Can you replace it?
(Clue: Look at both sides of the grid.)

NETWORK

Complete this puzzle by finishing off grids A and B, using the first grid as an example.

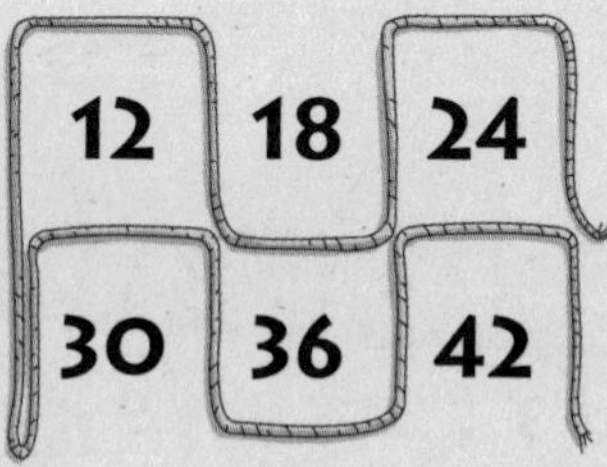

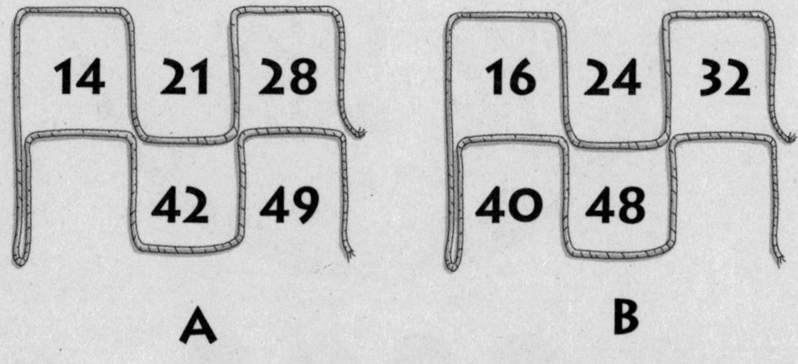

		4	6		5	3		1
1	5			4	7	8		
7		3				5		6
3				7	1		9	8
	4		9		3		1	
9	6		5	2				4
6		2				9		3
		9	2	8			5	7
5		8	1		9	4		

WHEEL SPIN

Which numbers are missing from the lower right circle?

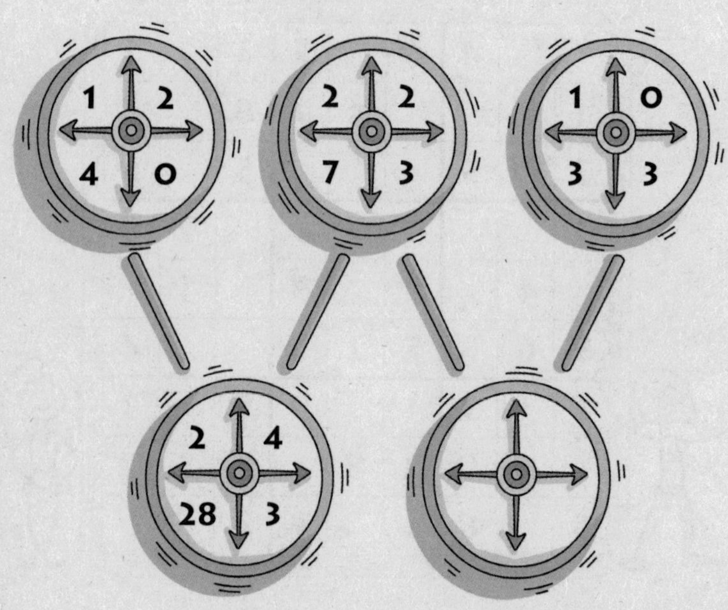

LEVEL 2

SPACE ODDITY

Look at this little boy's glasses very carefully and work out which number is the odd one out in each oval.

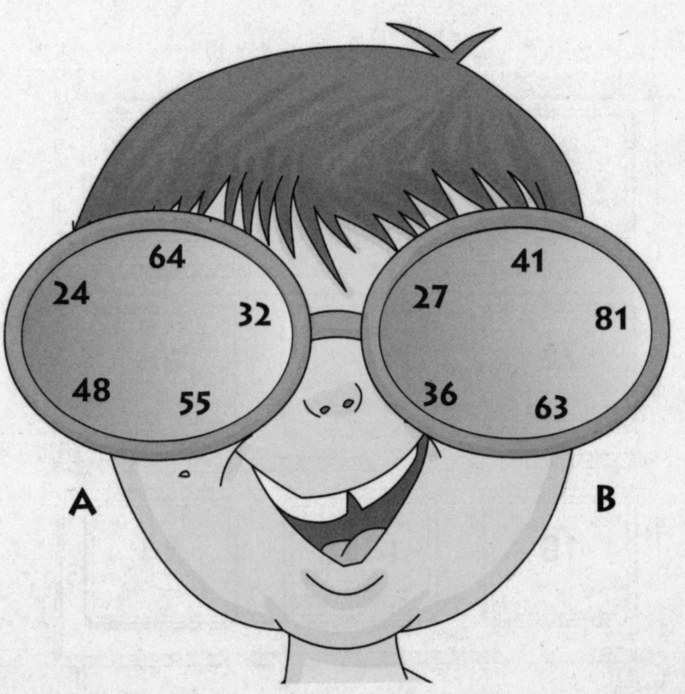

LEVEL 2

TAKE AWAY

What number goes in the middle square?
(Clue: It has got nothing to do with sums!)

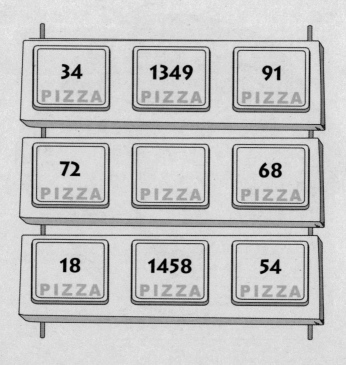

34 PIZZA	1349 PIZZA	91 PIZZA
72 PIZZA	PIZZA	68 PIZZA
18 PIZZA	1458 PIZZA	54 PIZZA

DOTTY!

Which of the bottom numbers will go into the centre dot?

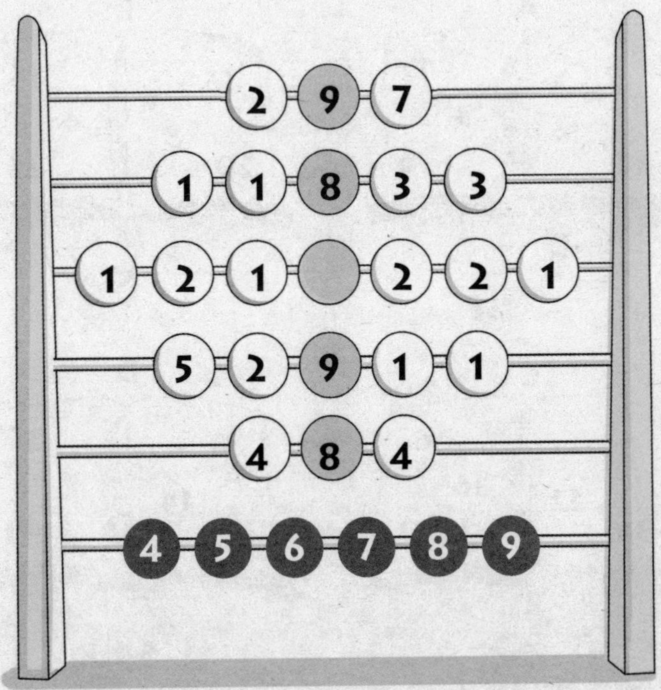

LEVEL 2

ROGUE NUMBER

In each book we have added a rogue number.
Can you work out which one it is?

A

9, 14, 18, 12, 3, 6

B

16, 8, 20, 14, 4, 24

C

24, 12, 36, 6, 16, 30

D

28, 14, 22, 35, 7, 42

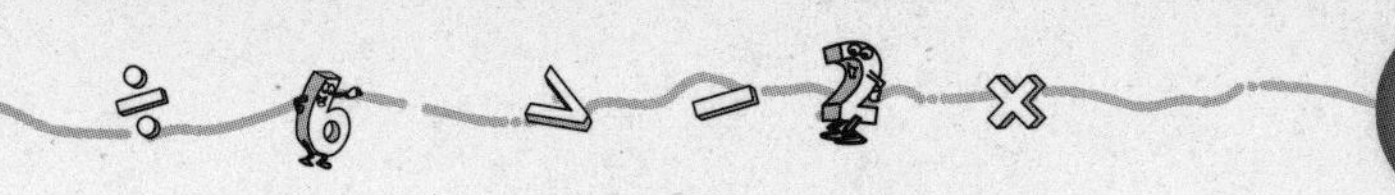

LEVEL 2

MISSING LINK

Which number completes this chain?

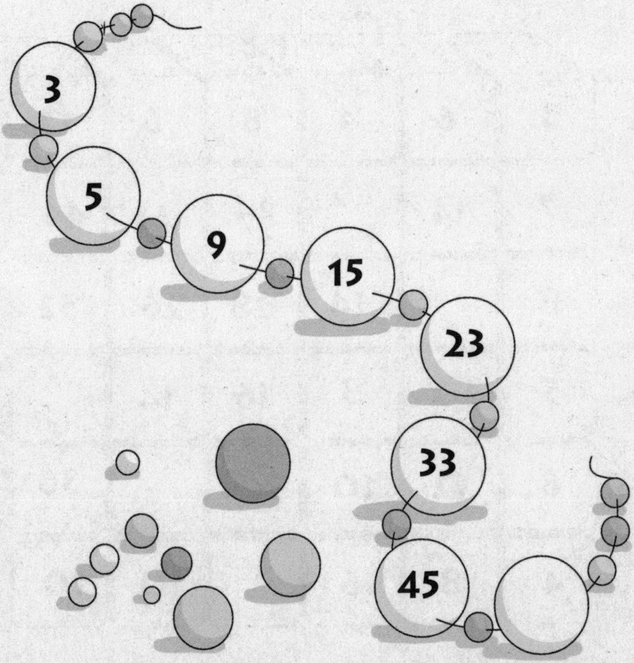

3

5

9

15

23

33

45

LINE UP

Using the same rule for every row, can you fill in the empty squares?

A	3	6	4	8	6	12
B	7	14		24	22	44
C	8		14	28	26	52
D	5	10	8	16	14	
E	6	12	10	20		36
F	4	8	6		10	20

CHANGE IT

Replace the question mark with the correct number.
(Clue: Look at the numbers within each segment.)

LEVEL 2

OPTIONS

Which of the three numbers at the bottom will complete this puzzle? (Clue: Try looking up and down.)

NUMBER SQUARE

By using every number between 1 and 16 can you complete this number square so that every line, up and down, left to right and diagonal adds up to 34?

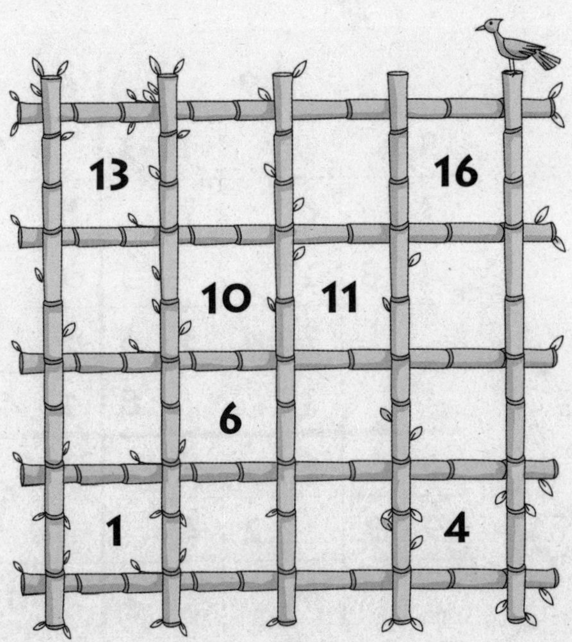

SUDOKU

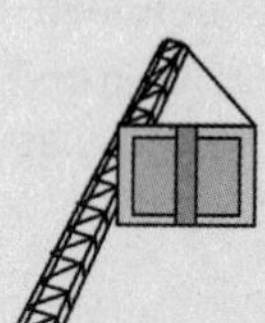

	2		9			6		
8				1	3		7	5
3		6		7		8		4
4	8	2	1			3		
		7	4	3	6	5		
		3			8	1	4	9
6		1		5		4		2
9	3		2	4				6
		4			7		1	

LEVEL 2

RING THE CHANGES

Which number goes in the empty ring?

43 21 12

63 81 45

11 90

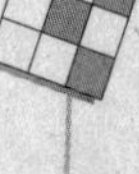

LEVEL 2

WHACKY WEB

Which number do you need to add in order to complete the web? (Clue: Try rotating the outer segments.)

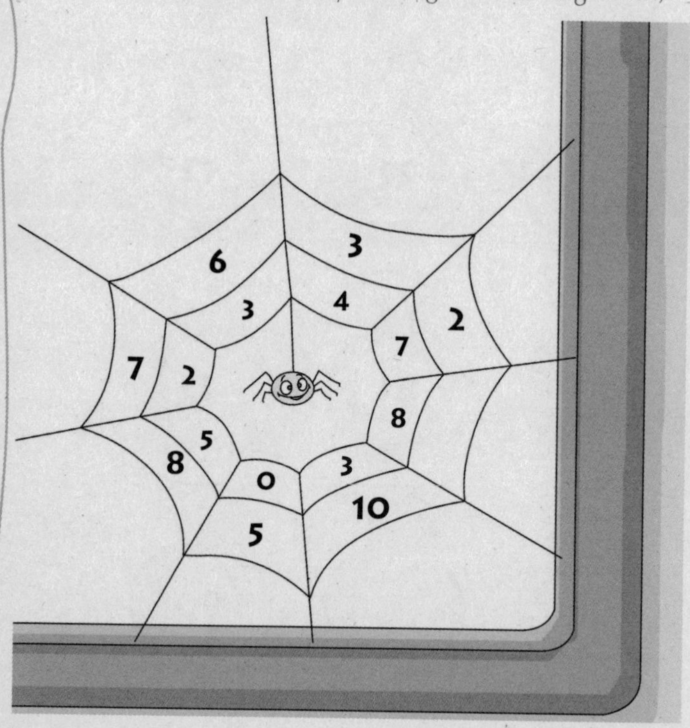

STAR STRUCK

Using the two completed stars as an example, work out what the missing number is in the third.

TRIO

Using the first two teddy bears as an example, fill in the empty space in the third.

7 4
14

9 4
18

5 6

GRID LOCK

Can you work out which numbers are required to complete grids A & B?

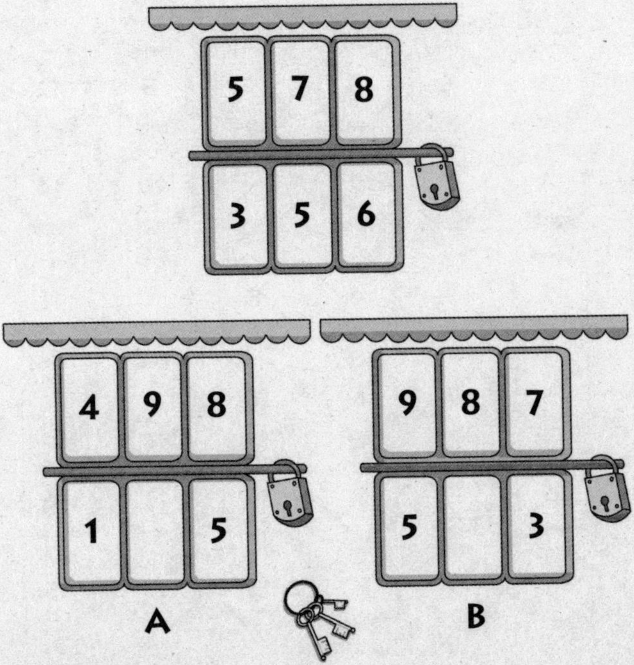

5	7	8
3	5	6

A

4	9	8
1		5

B

9	8	7
5		3

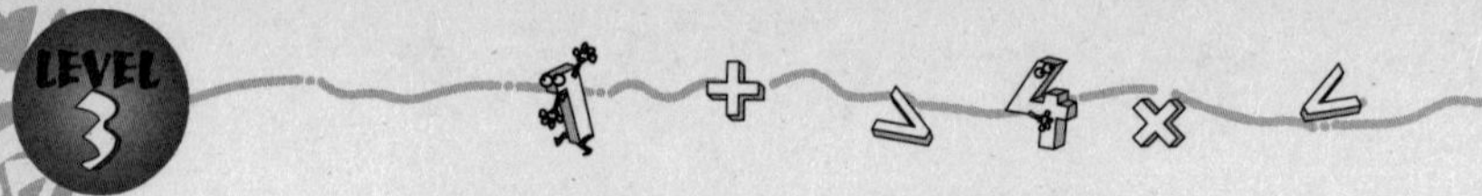

LINES OF THOUGHT

Put your thinking caps on and work out which number is missing from each line of octagons. Use the first line as an example.

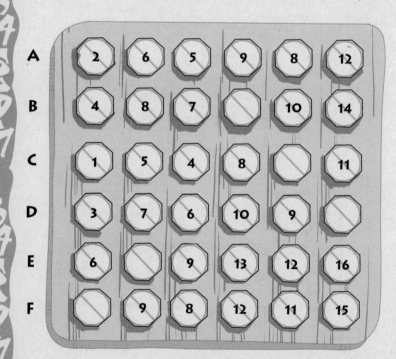

A	2	6	5	9	8	12
B	4	8	7		10	14
C	1	5	4	8		11
D	3	7	6	10	9	
E	6		9	13	12	16
F		9	8	12	11	15

PYRAMID POINTERS

Which number goes on the top point of pyramid C?

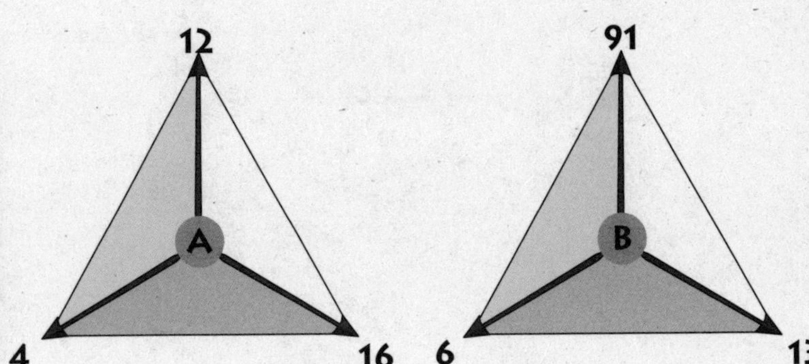

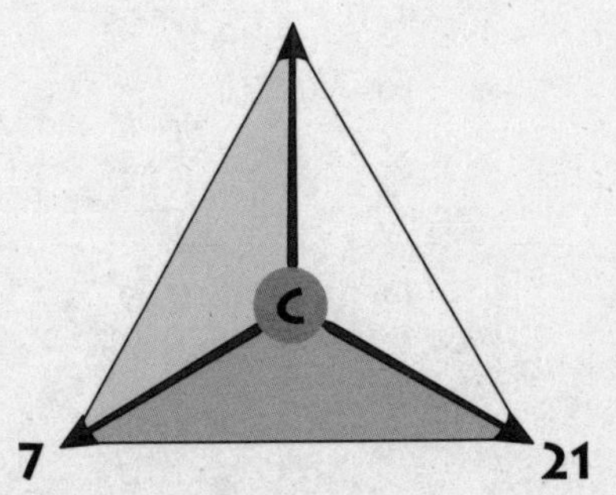

TIME OUT

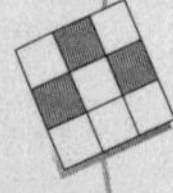

What time should be shown on the blank watch at the end?

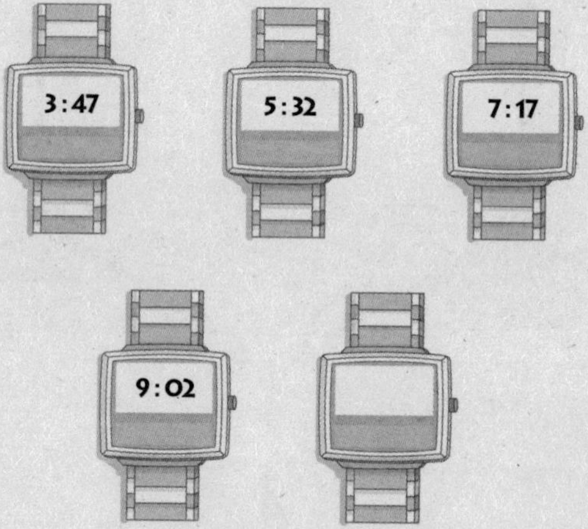

3:47	5:32	7:17
9:02	[blank]	

A	B	C	D
 11:32	10:32	11:17	10:47

LEVEL 3

SUDOKU

	6	4	2			8		
3			7		4		9	2
	9		5	8		7		3
	2	3	6					4
4		6	9		1	5		8
8					2	3	1	
9		8		4	7		6	
5	1		8		9			7
		7			5	1	8	

STAR STRUCK

Can you complete this puzzle?
(Clue: The lower two digits in each star are not what they seem.)

16
11 4
3 1

9
17 13
3 9

10
15 10
3

ODD ONE OUT

Which number is the odd one out in each wheel?

CRAZY CLOCKS

Look carefully at the sequence of clocks and fill in the blank.

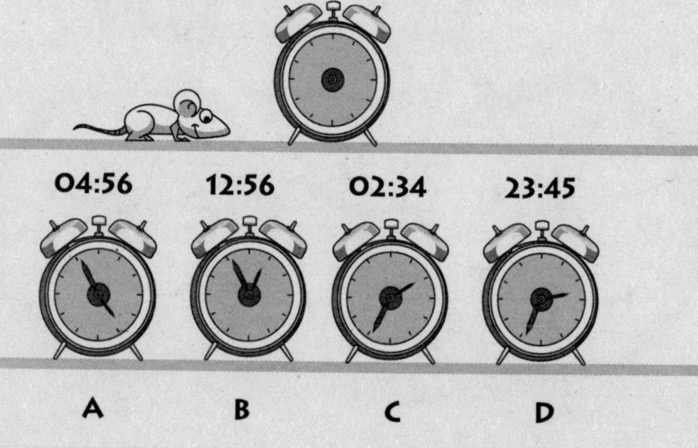

FIGURE-IT-OUT

Complete this puzzle by adding the correct number.
(Clue: Try looking at the puzzle from all directions.)

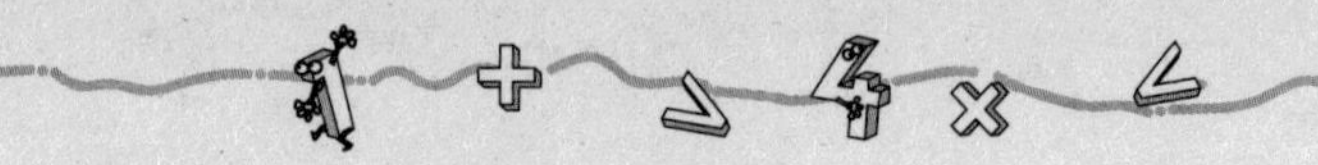

SLICED UP!

Can you work out which number is missing from the empty segment? (Clue: Look at the matching segments.)

DOTTY DOMINOES!

Which of the six spare dominoes completes this dotty sequence?

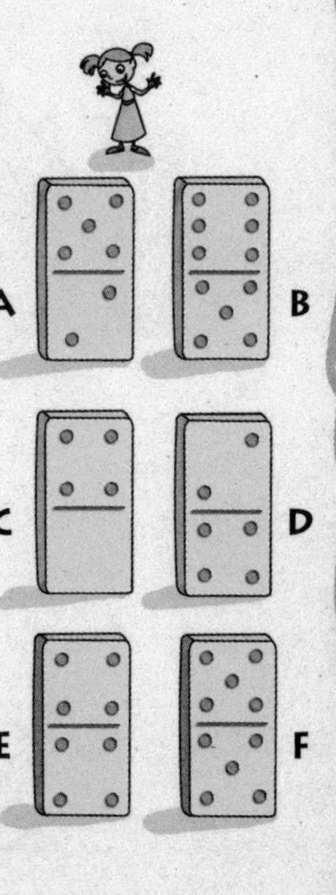

PYRAMID POSER

Work out which number goes at the top of the third pyramid?

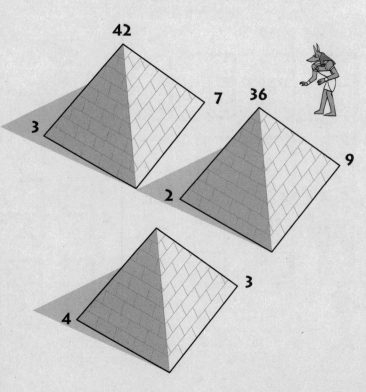

42

3 7

36

2 9

3

4

ALL SQUARE

Here is a complete puzzle - work out why it contains these numbers. (Clue: The centre square holds the answer.)

4	5	6	1
6	5	4	5
10	7	8	11
7	4	4	9

DOMINOES

By counting the dots on these dominoes, can you work out which of the six spare pieces completes the sequence?

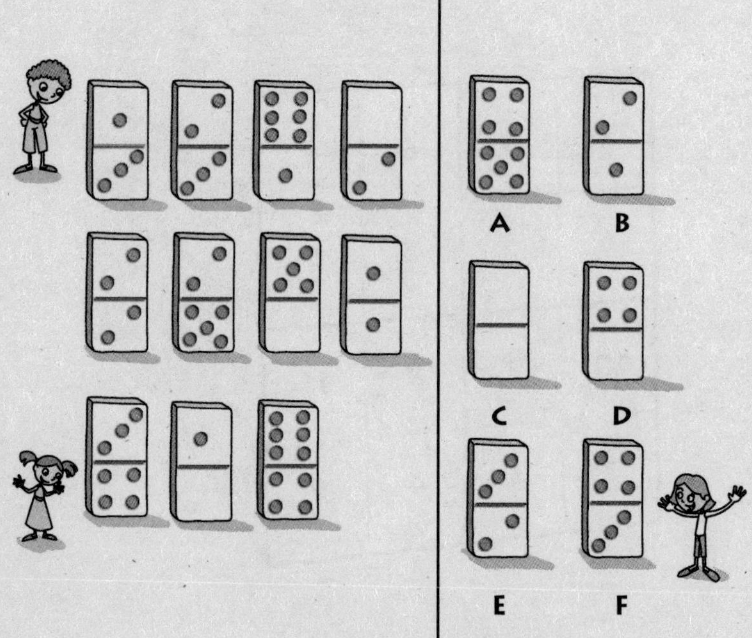

CROSS OVER

Which number is missing from each puzzle?

TRI - PIE

Which number is missing from the empty segment?
(Clue: Look at the matching segments on each circle.)

CIRCLES

Fill in the missing number.

DIGITAL DISCS

Using the first two discs as an example, fill in the empty segment.

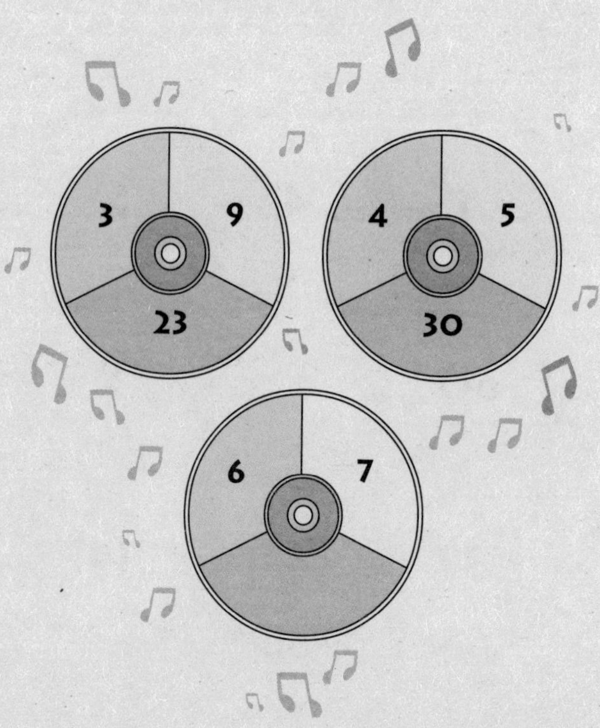

BOXING CLEVER

Can you work out which number is missing from the empty box?
(Clue: Look at each column separately.)

CHOCOLATE 1346	CHOCOLATE 2159	CHOCOLATE 1211
CHOCOLATE 2446	CHOCOLATE 3559	CHOCOLATE 2911
CHOCOLATE 3546	CHOCOLATE 4959	CHOCOLATE 4611
CHOCOLATE 4646	CHOCOLATE 6359	CHOCOLATE

FOUR SQUARE

Fill in the empty shape and complete the puzzle.
(Clue: Look carefully at the different shading to find the pattern.)

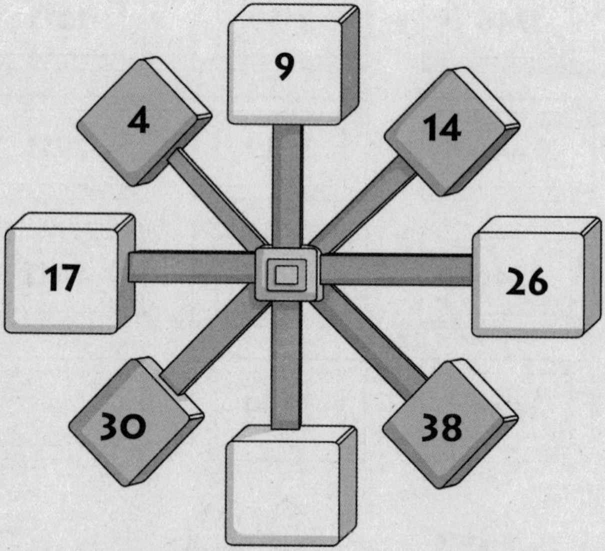

9

4

14

17

26

30

38

OUT OF PLACE

Which number doesn't go with the rest?

1

64

8

27

15

SUDOKU

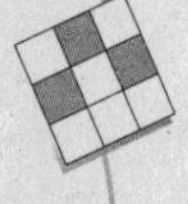

		4			5		7	9
	7		6	2	9		5	
	5	2			8	3	1	
8			9			1		7
	4	9	8		1	5	2	
5		6			7			4
	6	7	5			8	3	
	3		1	4	6		9	
1	9		7			6		

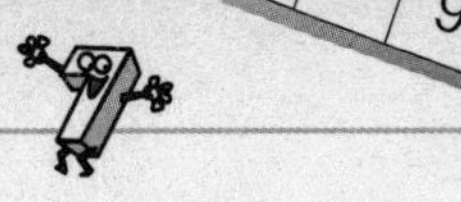

NUMBER BOX

Complete this number box by adding the correct number.
(Clue: The puzzle works up and down as well as side to side!)

2	6	3
8	48	
4	8	2

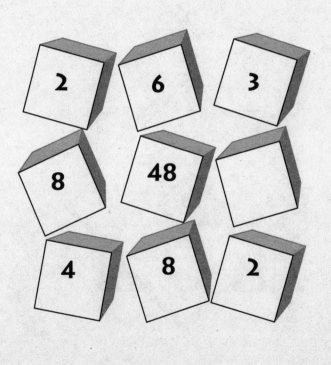

MAGIC SQUARE

Fill in the empty space and complete the puzzle.
(Clue: Look carefully at the grid to find the pattern.)

WEB WORLD

Which number replaces the question mark and completes the web?

LEVEL 3

ALL STAR

By using the first two stars as a guide, can you complete this puzzle?

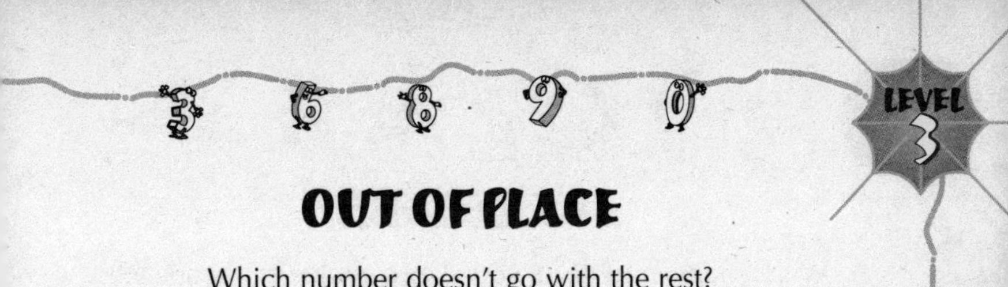

OUT OF PLACE

Which number doesn't go with the rest?

16

49

36

50

25

LEVEL 3

ET CETERA

Which number must be added to continue this sequence?

NUMBER WHEEL

Replace the question mark in this wheel with the correct number. (Clue: Look at the numbers in each segment as a group.)

SEQUENTIAL

Which number will complete this sequence?

3

7

15

31

HOLE IN ONE

We have left a hole in this puzzle. Can you fill it with the correct number? (Clue: Don't think in straight lines.)

CIRCLES

Which number is needed to finish the puzzle?

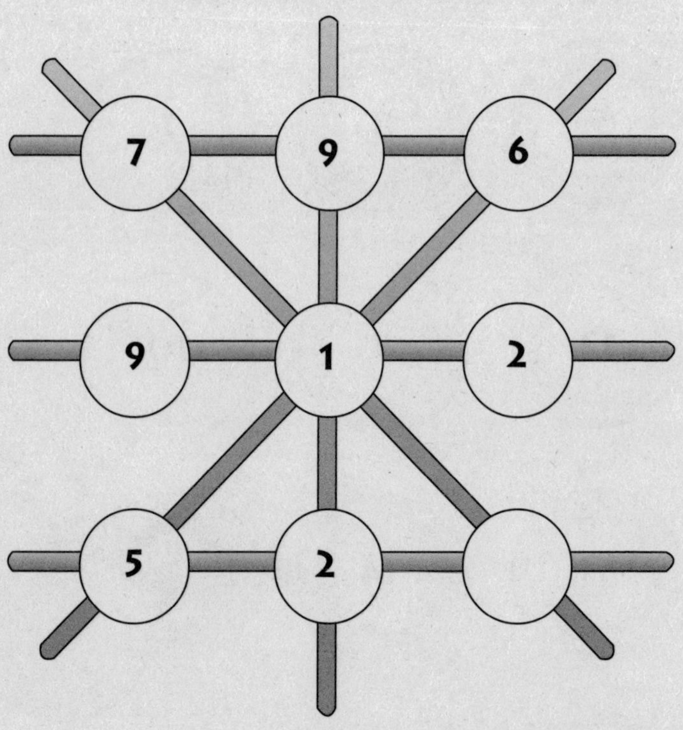

BOXING CLEVER

Which number completes this sequence?

MISSING NUMBERS

Which numbers are missing from the empty petals?
(Clue: Look at the matching segments,
the middle flower is the link!)

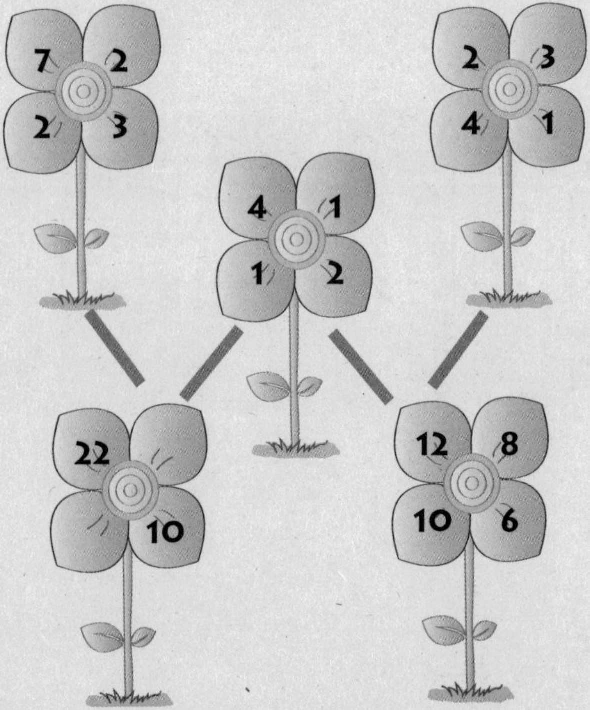

7 2
2 3

2 3
4 1

4 1
1 2

22
10

12 8
10 6

SUDOKU

1			7		6	3	2	4
7	9		4				8	
		4	2	5				1
2		7		6			4	
	1		8		5		3	
	3			4		5		6
5				8	3	2		
	2				7		6	9
6	7	1	9		4			3

HONEYCOMB

Which number is the odd one out?

LEVEL 3

HOLE NUMBERS

Complete this puzzle by adding the correct number to the empty circle. (Clue: Straight thinking will not help you with this one!)

MAGIC SQUARE

By using every number between 1 and 16 can you complete this number square so that every line, up and down, left to right and diagonal adds up to 34?

MISFITS

One number in each kite is a misfit - in other words it doesn't follow the same rules or requirements as all the others. Can you work out which one it is?

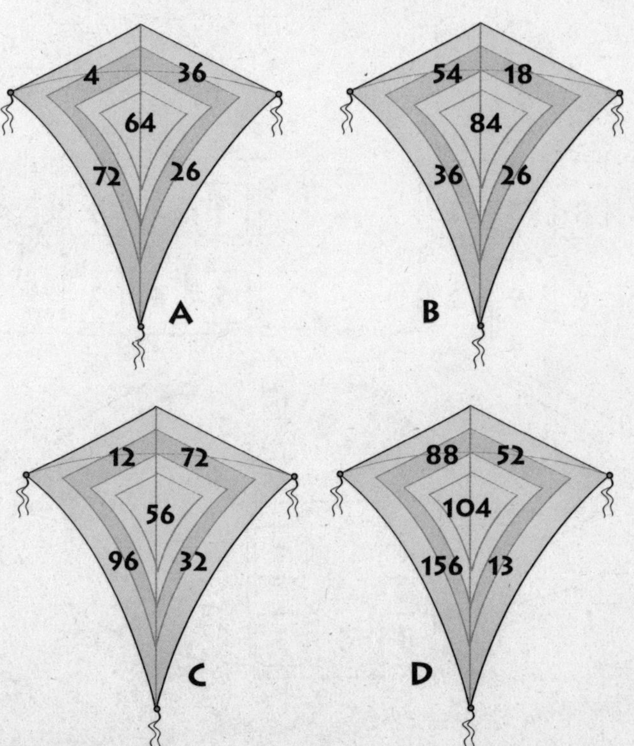

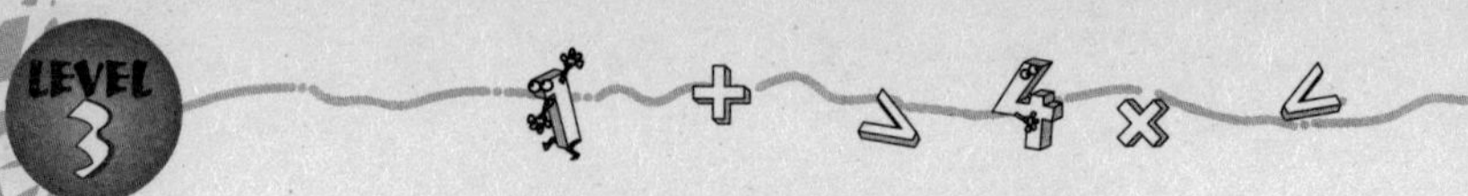

HOUSEY HOUSEY!

Using the first two houses as an example, can you work out which number is missing from the third house?

9

3 7

6 9 2

11

1 9

5 6 2

4 1

8 6 3

OPTIONAL EXTRAS

Which of the three optional extra numbers at the bottom will replace the question mark?

(Clue: Don't just look from left to right.)

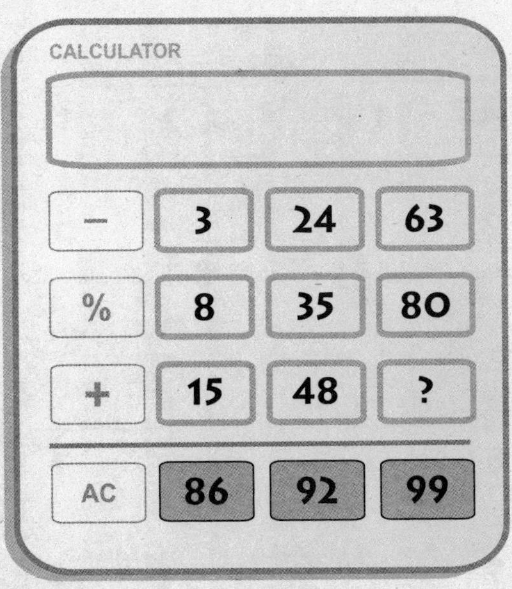

NUMBER SQUARE

This puzzle is a little bit different in that we have given you all the numbers already to show you what the finished teaser looks like. Can you work out why these numbers are correct?

(Clue: The centre square is the key.)

4 1
3

2 1
0

15 8
12 3

6
5 4

7
1 4

FIGURE-IT-OUT

Which four-figure answer is missing from the empty box?

SUDOKU

8		4	6				5	
5				9	7	3		6
	3	6	5				1	
1		9	8		4	7		2
	6			2			9	
2		8	3		9	5		1
	8				1	6	4	
4		3	2	5				9
	7				8	1		3

SHAPE UP

Find the missing number to complete the puzzle.

Top left: 5 (top), 3 (left), 9 (right), 7 (bottom)

Top right: 8 (top), 2 (left), 4 (right), 10 (bottom)

Bottom left: 11 (top), 9 (left), 1 (right), 3 (bottom)

Bottom right: 6 (top), 5 (left), ? (right), 8 (bottom)

LEVEL 3

TAKE AWAY

What number goes in the middle rectangle?
(Clue: It has got nothing to do with sums!)

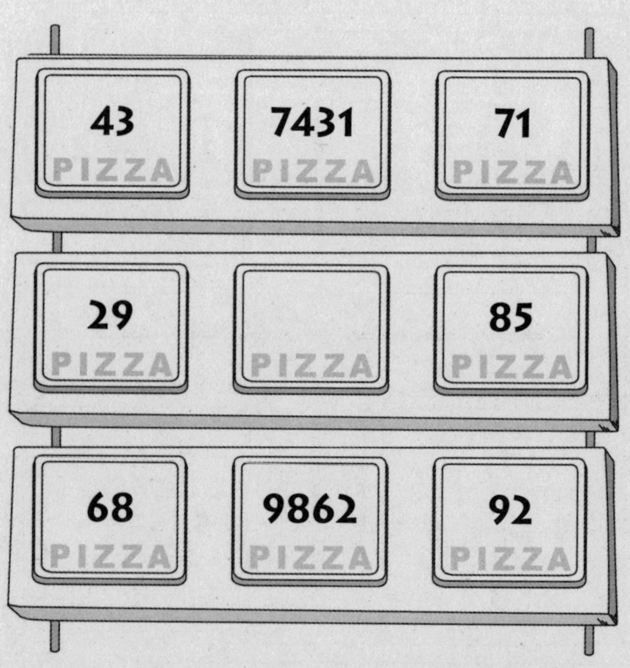

DOTTY!

Which of the bottom numbers will go into the centre dot?

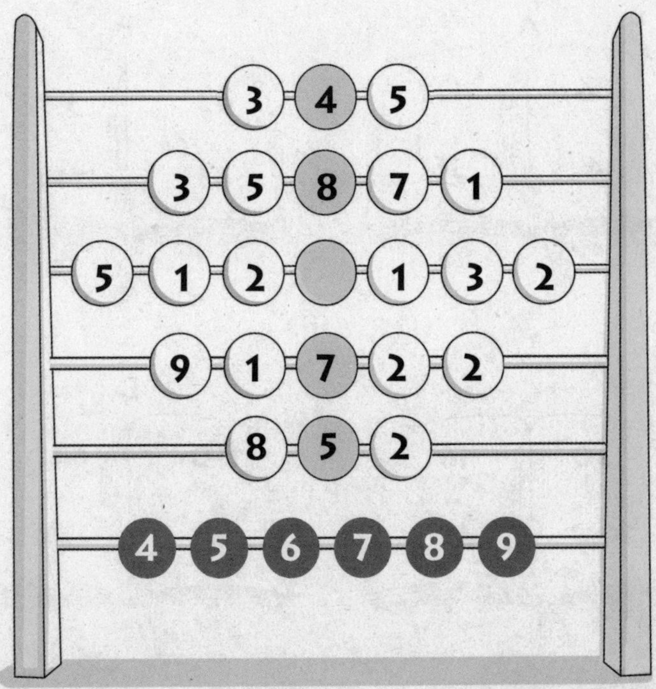

ROGUE NUMBER

In each square we have added a rogue number.
Can you work out which one it is?

A

86	121
4	36

B

42	9
81	144

C

130	16
100	49

D

110	64
25	225

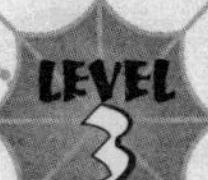

MISSING LINK

Which number completes this chain?

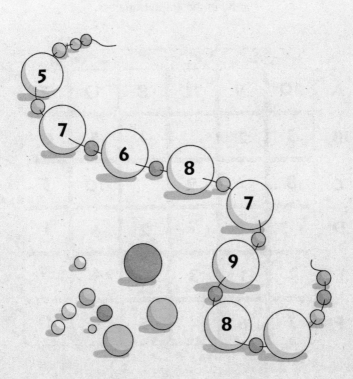

5

7

6

8

7

9

8

LEVEL 3

LINE UP

Using the same rule for every row, can you fill in the empty squares?

A	10	9	11	8	12	7
B	3	2		1	5	0
C	8	7	9		10	5
D		3	5	2	6	1
E	2	1	3		4	-1
F	7	6		5	9	4

STAR STRUCK

Using the two completed stars as an example, find the missing number.

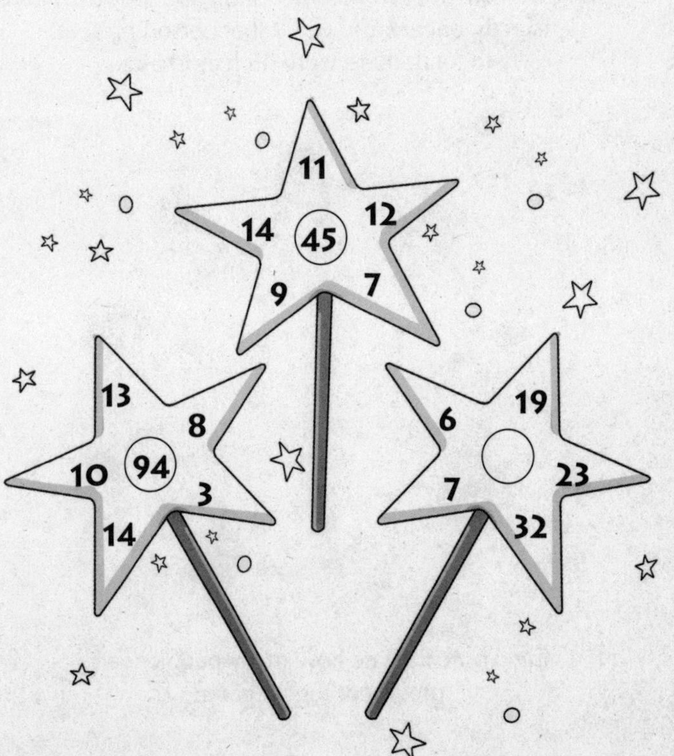

MINDBENDER

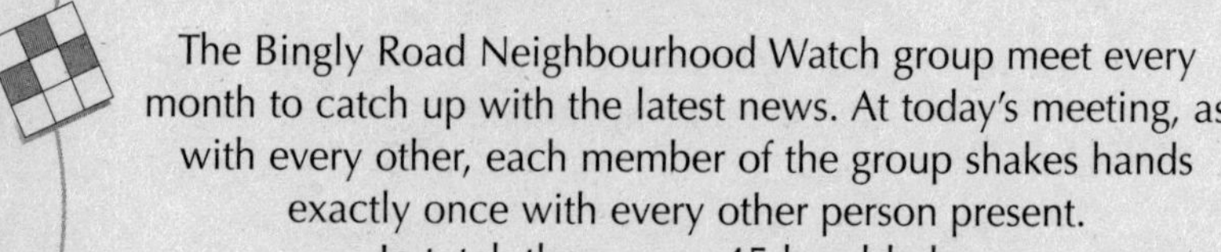

The Bingly Road Neighbourhood Watch group meet every month to catch up with the latest news. At today's meeting, as with every other, each member of the group shakes hands exactly once with every other person present. In total, there were 45 handshakes.

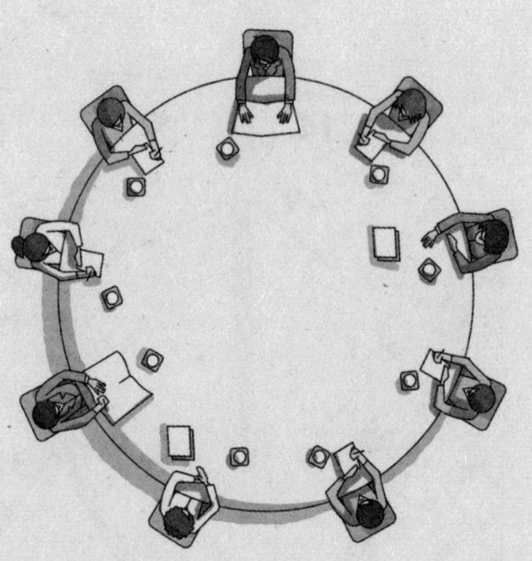

Can you calculate how many people were present at the meeting?

SUDOKU

3			2	9		6		1
	5	2			7	9	8	4
7		1		4			5	
			5	8			2	
4	7	6				8	3	5
	2			3	6			
	6			5		4		3
2	4	9	1			5	6	
5		8		6	9			7

NUMBER WINDOW

Work out which number is missing and complete the puzzle.

3	6	4	3
8	16	8	6
10	5	4	2
6	3	16	?

LEVEL 3

GONE MISSING!

The number in the middle column has gone missing.
Can you replace it?
(Clue: Look at both sides of the grid.)

2 4 6 8 10 12

NETWORK

Complete this puzzle by finishing off grids A and B, using the first grid as an example.

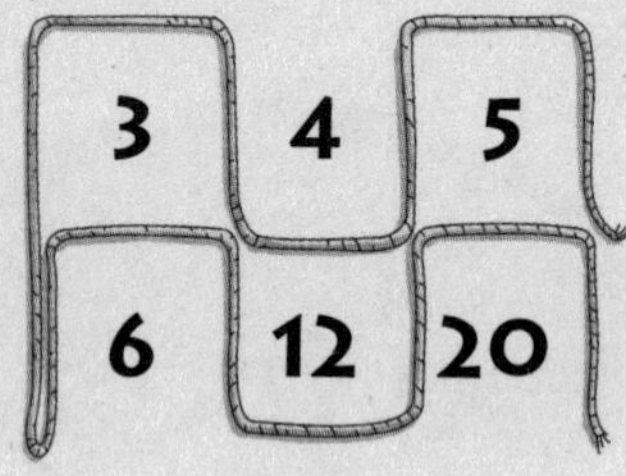

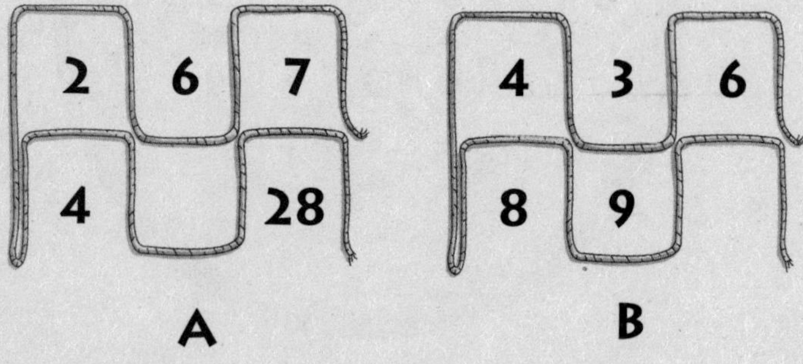

LEVEL 3

CHANGE IT

Replace the question mark with the correct number.
(Clue: Look at the numbers within each segment.)

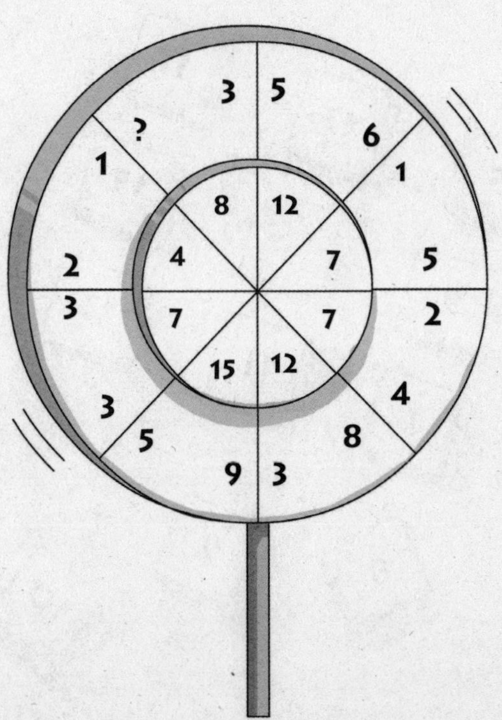

OPTIONS

Which of the three numbers at the bottom will complete this puzzle? (Clue: Try looking up and down.)

11
13
5
15
9
13
11
7

8
9
10

LEVEL 3

NUMBER SQUARE

By using every number between 1 and 16 can you complete this number square so that every line, up and down, left to right and diagonal adds up to 34?

WHEEL SPIN

Which numbers are missing from the last wheel?
(Clue: Move up and down to get the answer.)

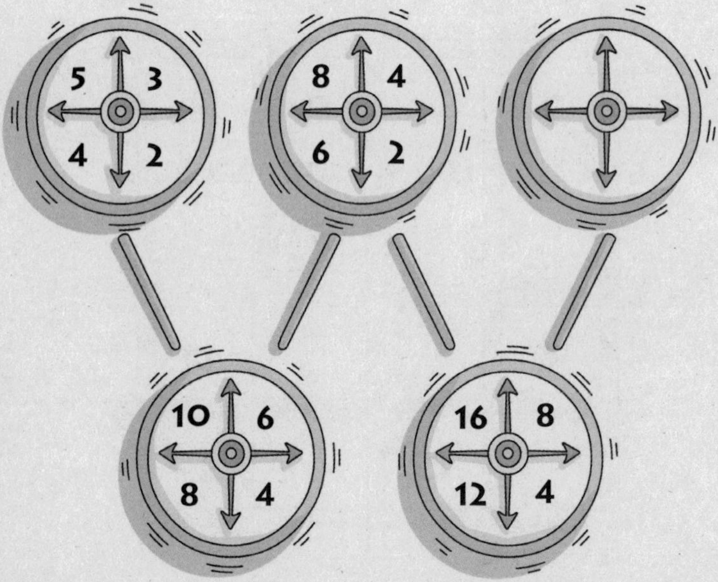

5	3
4	2

8	4
6	2

10	6
8	4

16	8
12	4

LEVEL 3

SPACE ODDITY

Look at this little boy's glasses very carefully and work out which number is the odd one out in each oval.

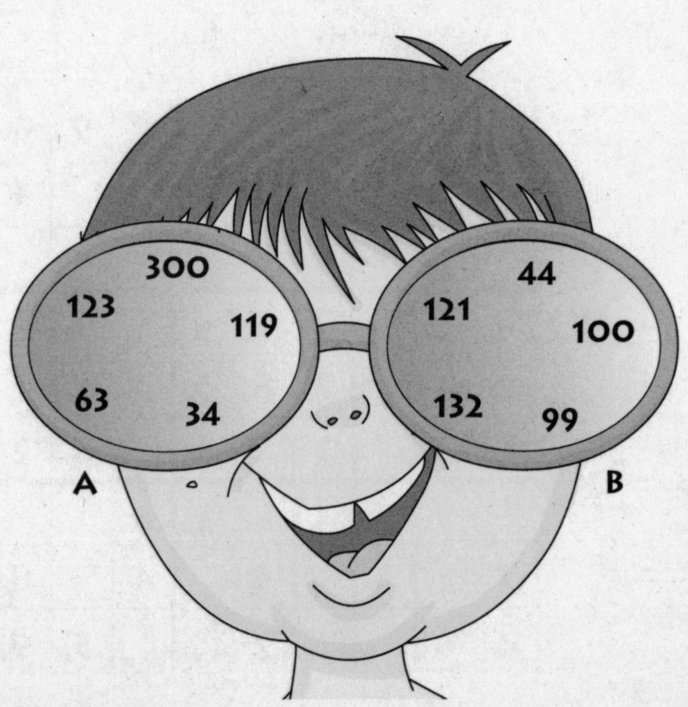

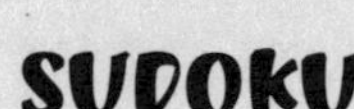

SUDOKU

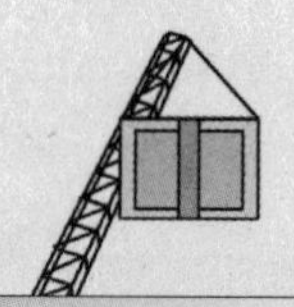

6	4			7			9	3
3		5		4		7		1
		9	1		3	5		
8	3		2		4		7	5
		4	7	8	5	3		
1	5		3		6		4	2
		8	4		1	6		
7		2		6		4		8
4	6			2			5	9

RING THE CHANGES

Which number goes in the empty ring?

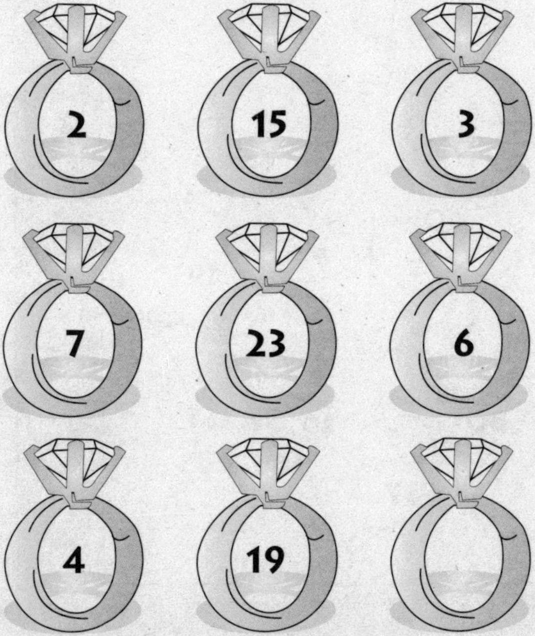

2	15	3
7	23	6
4	19	

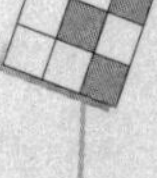

LEVEL 3

WHACKY WEB

Which number do you need to add in order to complete the web?

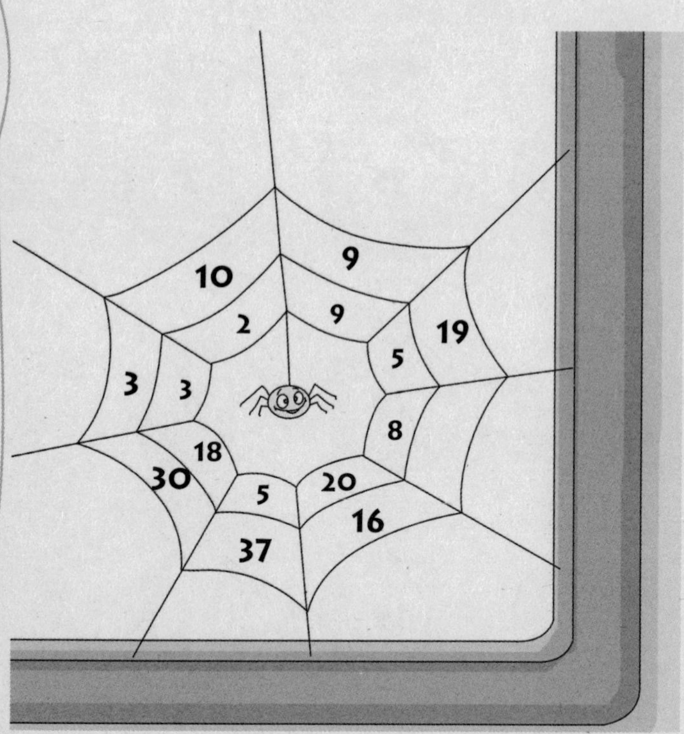

STAR STRUCK

Using the two completed stars as an example, work out what the missing number is in the third.

TRIO

Using the first two teddy bears as an example, fill in the empty space in the third.

8 3
42

9 6
45

2 7

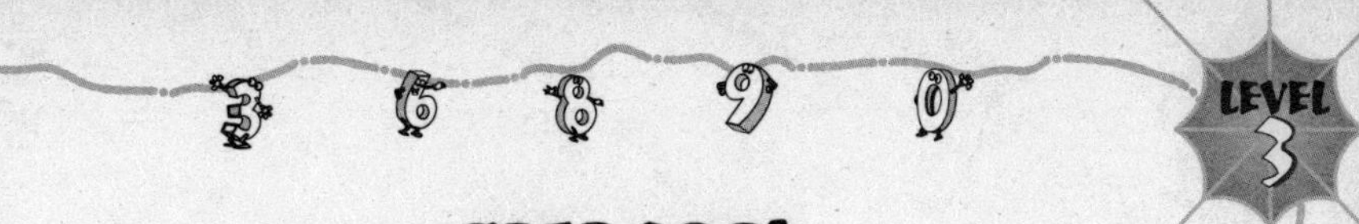

GRID LOCK

Can you work out which numbers are required to complete grids A & B?

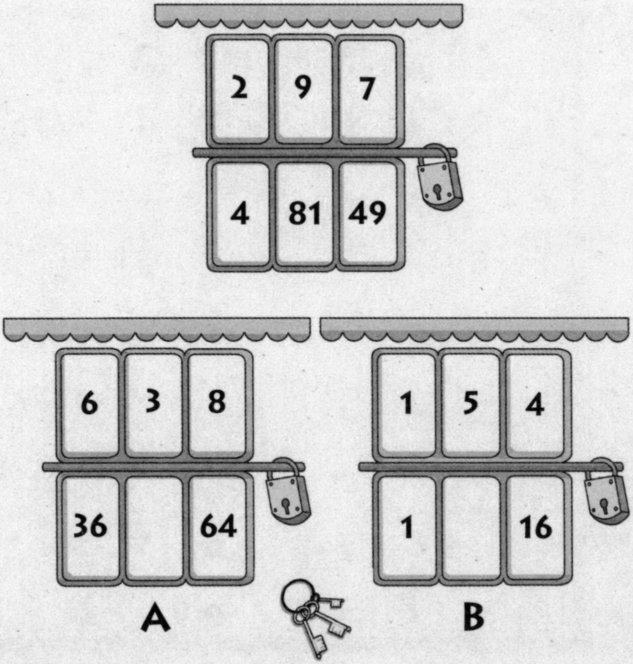

2	9	7
4	81	49

6	3	8
36		64

A

1	5	4
1		16

B

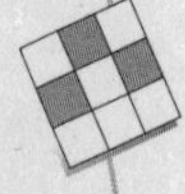

SUDOKU

	1		5		9	2		
	9	4	6		7	1		5
2				8			3	
4	8				2	7		
	6	5		7		4	1	
		3	1				9	6
	4			5				1
1		8	7		6	5	2	
		2	3		4		6	

LINES OF THOUGHT

Put your thinking cap on and work out which number is missing from each line of octagons. Use the first line as an example.

A	2	3	7	12	21	35
B		4	7	13	22	37
C	3		9	15	26	43
D	1	1	4	7		22
E	1	2	5		16	27
F	1	3		11	19	32

PYRAMID POINTERS

Which number goes on the top point of pyramid C?

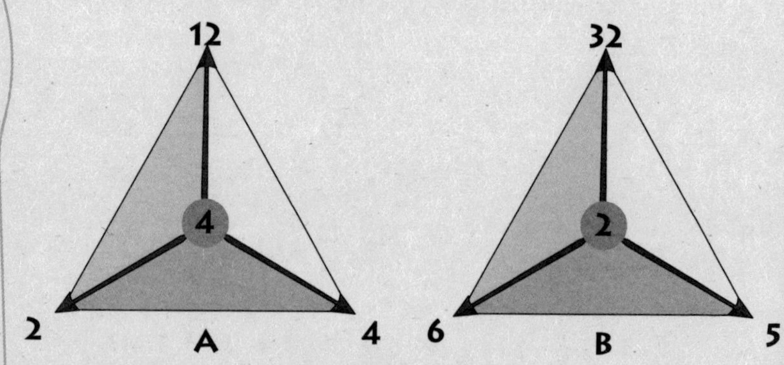

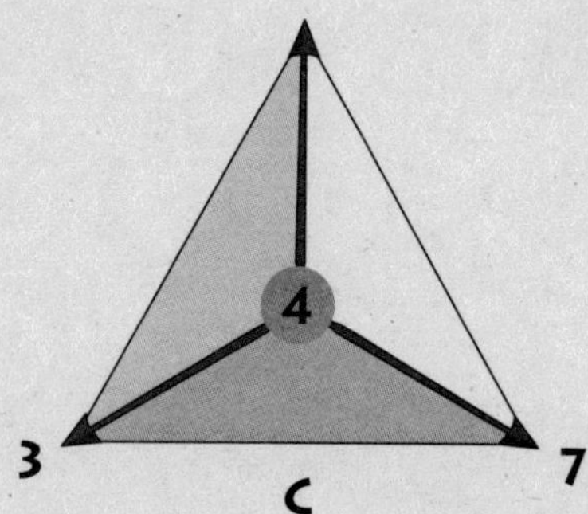

TIME OUT

What time should be shown on the blank watch at the end?

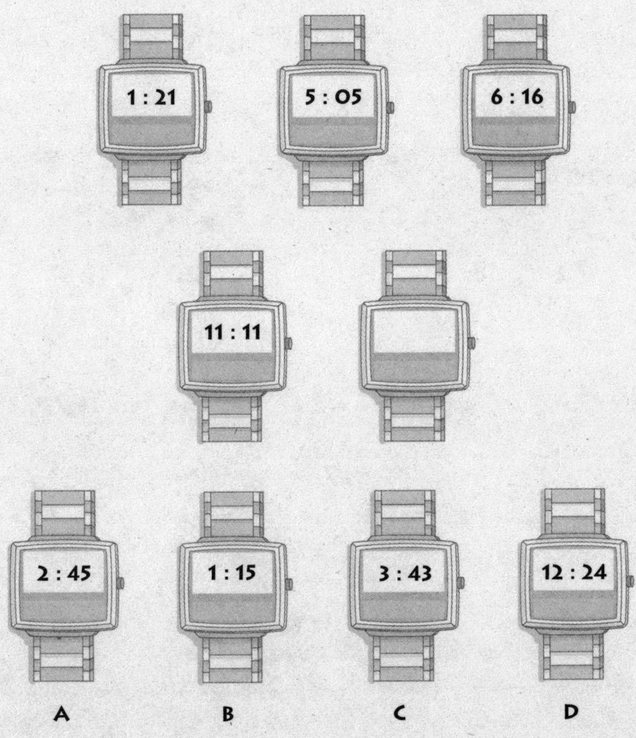

LEVEL 4

STAR STRUCK

Can you complete this puzzle by using the first two stars as a guide?

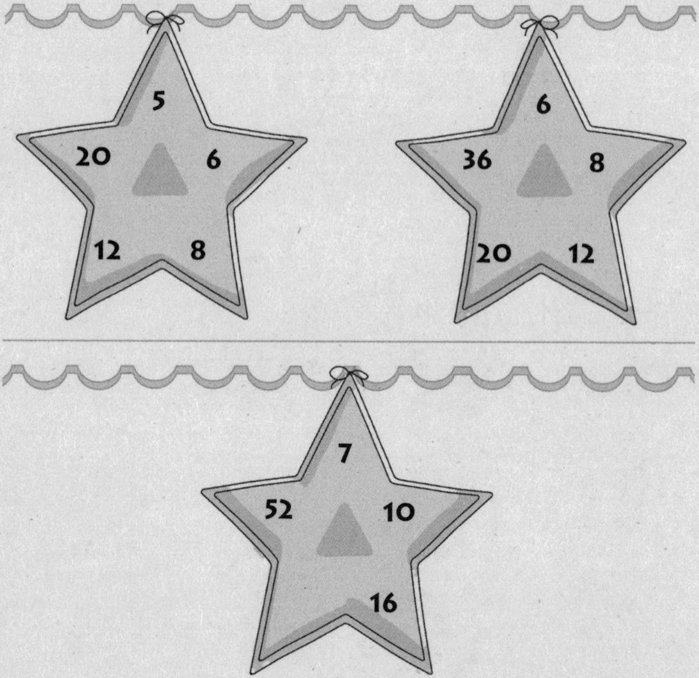

5
20 6
12 8

6
36 8
20 12

7
52 10
16

FIGURE IT OUT

Complete this puzzle by adding the correct number.
(Clue: Try looking at the puzzle from all directions.)

8	3	4
1	5	9
6	7	

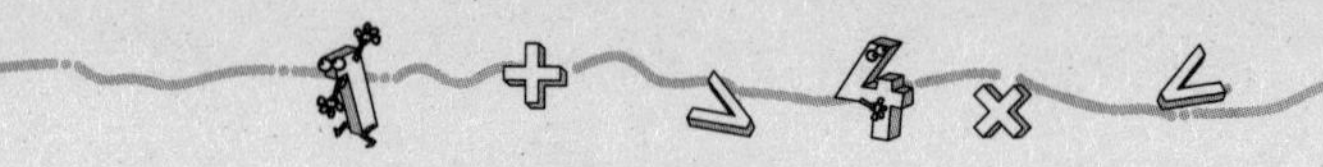

SLICED UP!

Can you work out which number is missing from the empty segment? (Clue: Look at matching segments.)

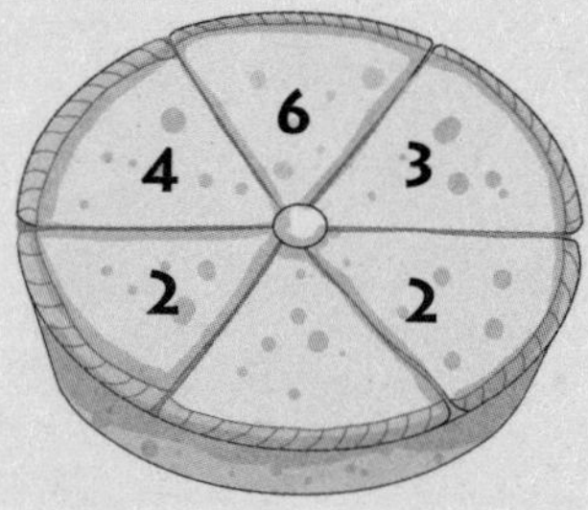

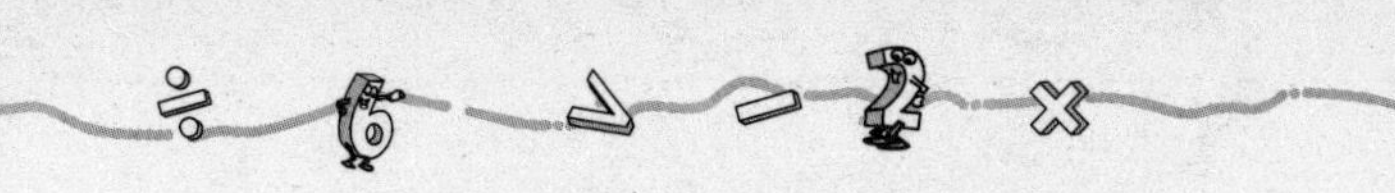

LEVEL 4

DOTTY DOMINOES!

Which of the six spare dominoes completes this dotty sequence?

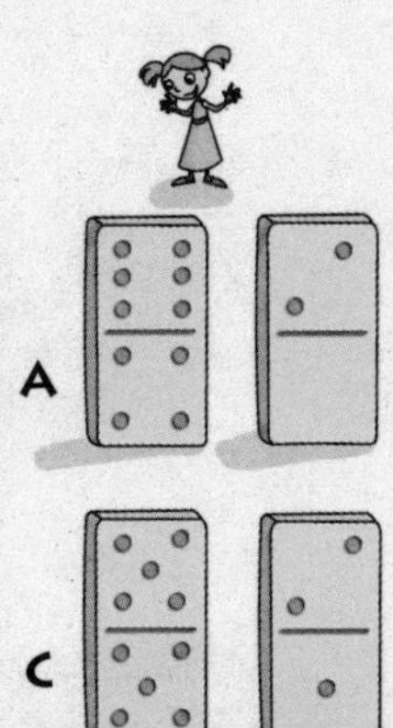

ODD ONE OUT

Which number is the odd one out in each wheel?

A: 63, 9, 18, 27, 35, 72, 45

B: 48, 36, 84, 26, 12, 72, 60

SUDOKU

4		1			2	8	5	
	2	6		5	7			9
	9		8		3	1		
6				7	8			4
3		8		1		2		6
7			2	6				5
		4	7		1		2	
1			4	2		6	9	
	8	5	9			7		1

CRAZY CLOCKS

Look carefully at the sequence of clocks and fill in the blank.

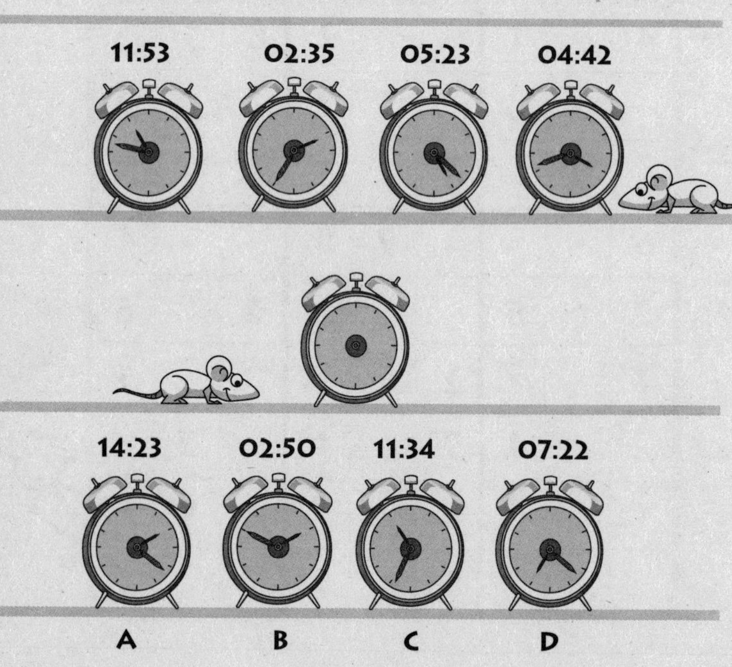

PYRAMID POSER

Work out which number goes at the top of the third pyramid.

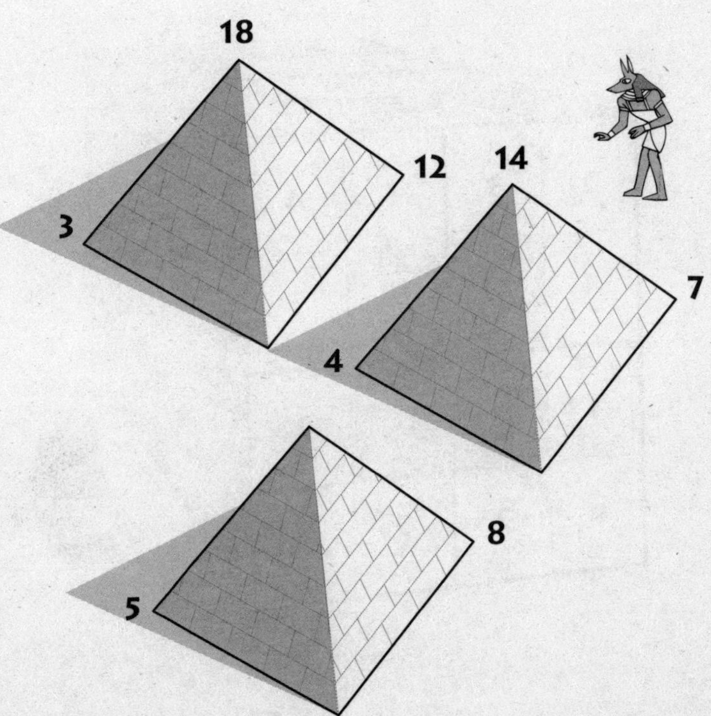

ALL SQUARE

Here is a complete puzzle - work out why it contains these numbers. (Clue: The centre square holds the answer.)

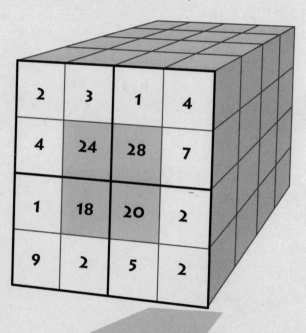

2	3	1	4
4	24	28	7
1	18	20	2
9	2	5	2

DOMINOES

By counting the dots on these dominoes, can you work out which of the six spare pieces completes the sequence?

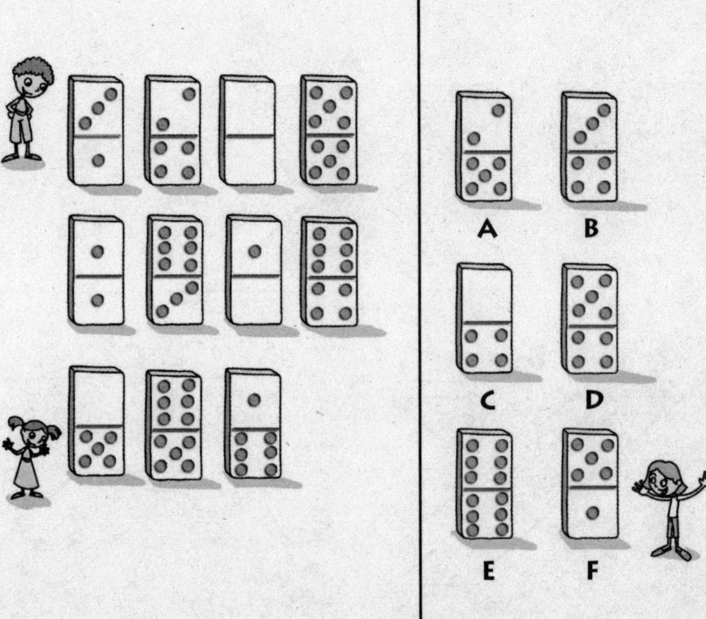

CROSS OVER

Which number is missing from each puzzle?

LEVEL 4

CIRCLES

Fill in the missing number.

3	6	10
45	55	15
36		21

DIGITAL DISCS

Using the first two discs as an example, fill in the empty segment.

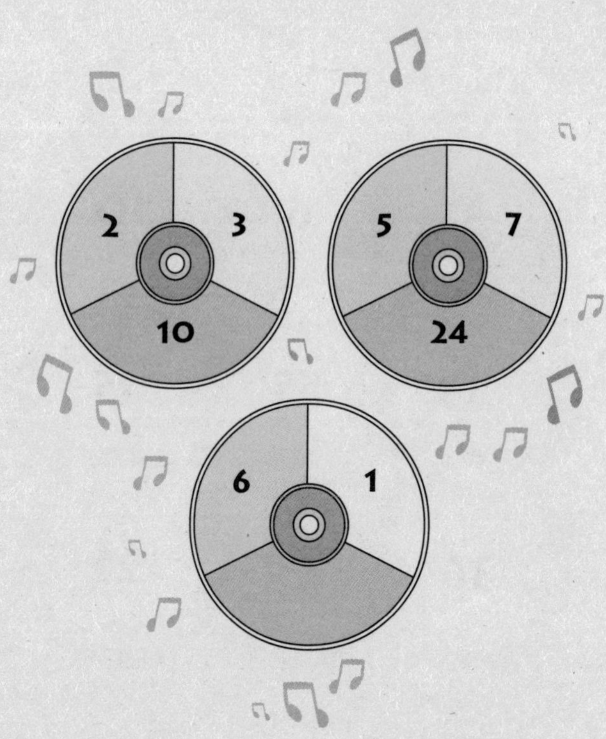

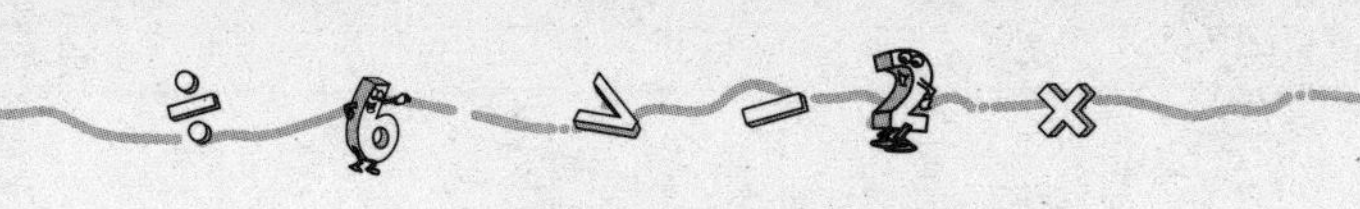

LEVEL 4

BOXING CLEVER

Can you work out which numbers are missing from the box on the bottom right? (Clue: Look at each row.)

CHOCOLATE 1515	CHOCOLATE 2109	CHOCOLATE 0624
CHOCOLATE 2015	CHOCOLATE 1718	CHOCOLATE 3203
CHOCOLATE 3505	CHOCOLATE 1030	CHOCOLATE 2713
CHOCOLATE 0936	CHOCOLATE 1332	CHOCOLATE 25??

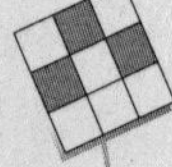

SUDOKU

5			9		8		3	
1		9	2				6	4
		7		3	1	2	9	
2		5		8			7	
4			6	9	5			8
	6			4		9		1
	2	8	5	1		6		
3	5				6	7		9
	1		3		4			2

LEVEL 4

FOUR SQUARE

Fill in the empty shape and complete the puzzle.
(Clue: Look carefully at the different shading to find the pattern.)

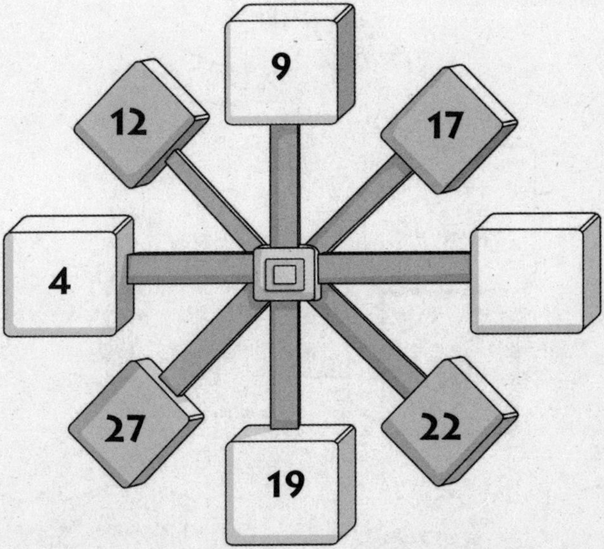

9
12
17
4
27
22
19

OUT OF PLACE

Which number doesn't go with the rest?

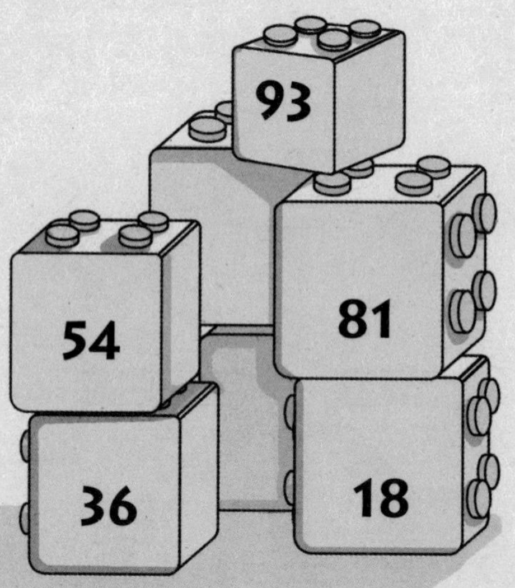

ET CETERA

Which number must be added to continue this sequence?

TRI - PIE

Which number is missing from the empty segment?
(Clue: Look at the matching segments on each circle.)

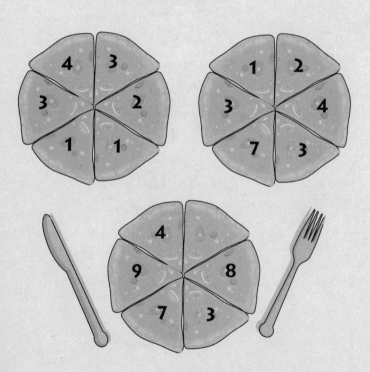

4 3
3 2
1 1

1 2
3 4
7 3

4
9 8
7 3

NUMBER BOX

Complete this number box by adding the correct number in the empty box.
(Clue: The puzzle works up and down as well as side to side!)

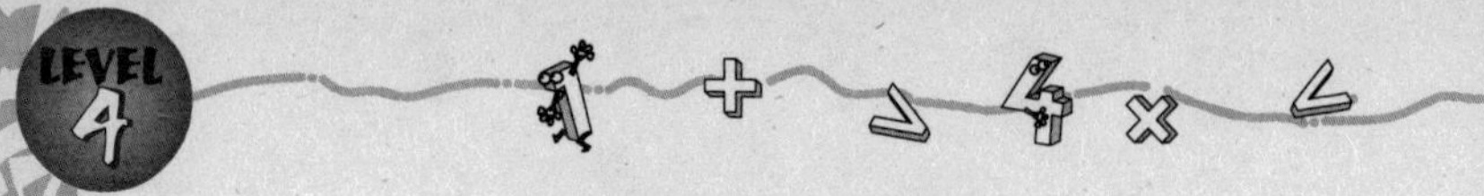

WEB WORLD

Which number replaces the question mark and completes the web?

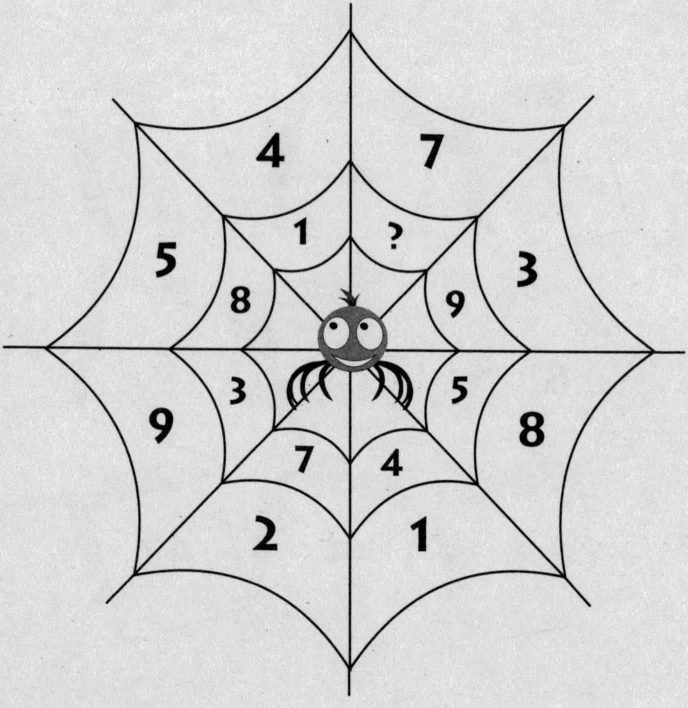

4 7

1 ?

5 3

8 9

3 5

9 8

7 4

2 1

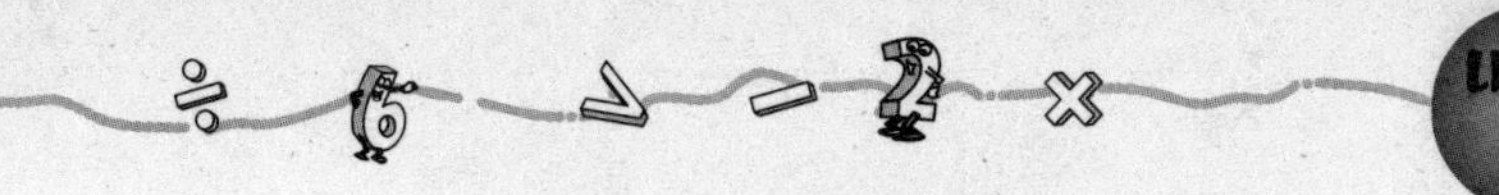

MAGIC SQUARE

Fill in the empty space and complete the puzzle.
(Clue: Look carefully at the grid to find the pattern.)

2

1 4

1 24 3

6

4

SUDOKU

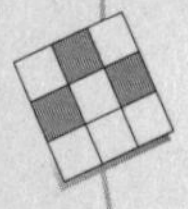

		2	9	6	5	1		
	5				8			9
8		9			3	2		4
	4			3	1		8	5
1		6		9		7		3
9	3		8	2			6	
7		3	4			5		2
6			3				1	
		8	1	7	9	3		

ALL STAR

By using the first two stars as a guide, can you complete this puzzle?

CIRCLES

Which number is needed to finish the puzzle?

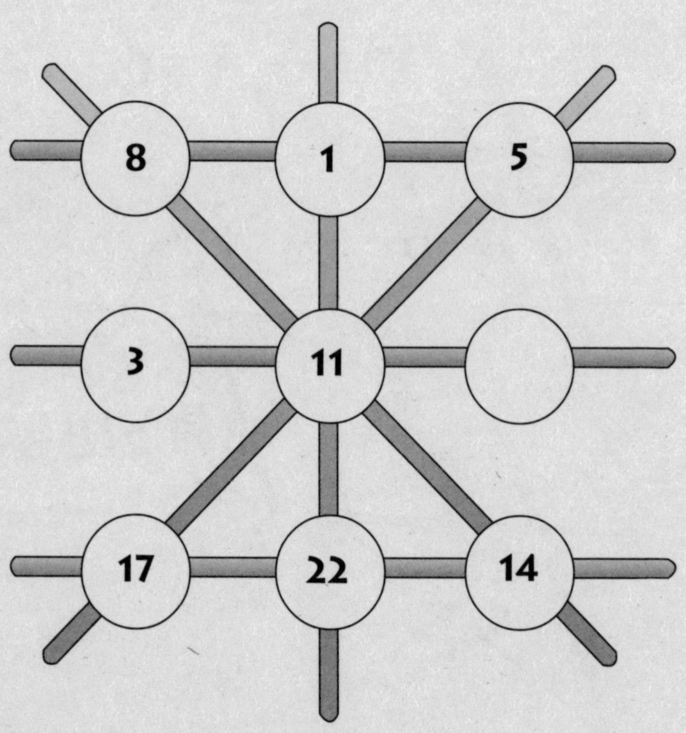

BOXING CLEVER

Which number completes this sequence?

LEVEL 4

NUMBER WHEEL

Replace the question mark in this wheel with the correct number. (Clue: Pair up each outer number with an inner number.)

SEQUENTIAL

Which number will complete this sequence?

3

10

24

52

HOLE IN ONE

We have left a hole in this puzzle. Can you fill it with the correct number? (Clue: Don't think in straight lines.)

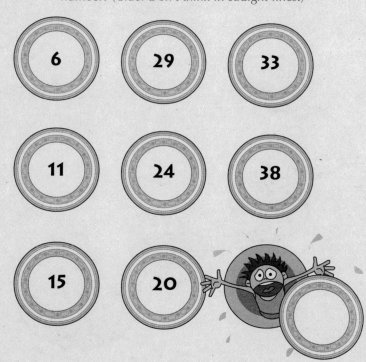

6	29	33
11	24	38
15	20	

MAGIC SQUARE

By using every number between 1 and 25 can you complete this number square so that every line, up and down, left to right and diagonal adds up to 65?

MISFITS

One number in each kite is a misfit, in other words it doesn't follow the same rules or requirements as all the others. Can you work out which one it is?

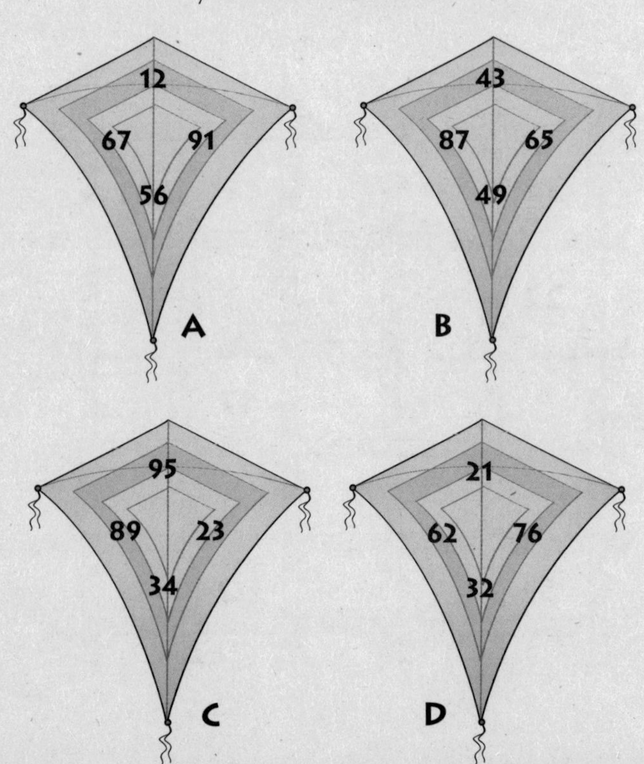

HOUSEY HOUSEY!

Using the first two houses as an example, can you work out which number is missing from the third house?

3

4 7

2 4 4

9

8 2

3 6 8

6

3 4

7 5

OPTIONAL EXTRAS

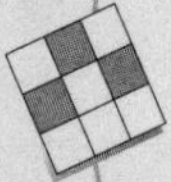

Which of the three optional extra numbers at the bottom will replace the question mark?
(Clue: Don't just look from left to right.)

CALCULATOR

–	5	7	11
%	35	25	17
+	47	61	?
AC	72	77	84

SUDOKU

6			4	7		2		
9	4		1				7	3
	5		2	9	8		4	
		1		4	2			7
2	6						9	4
8			5	3		6		
	3		8	6	7		2	
5	8				4		3	1
		7		1	5			8

MISSING NUMBERS

Which numbers are missing from the empty petals?
(Clue: Look at the matching segments,
the middle flower is the link!)

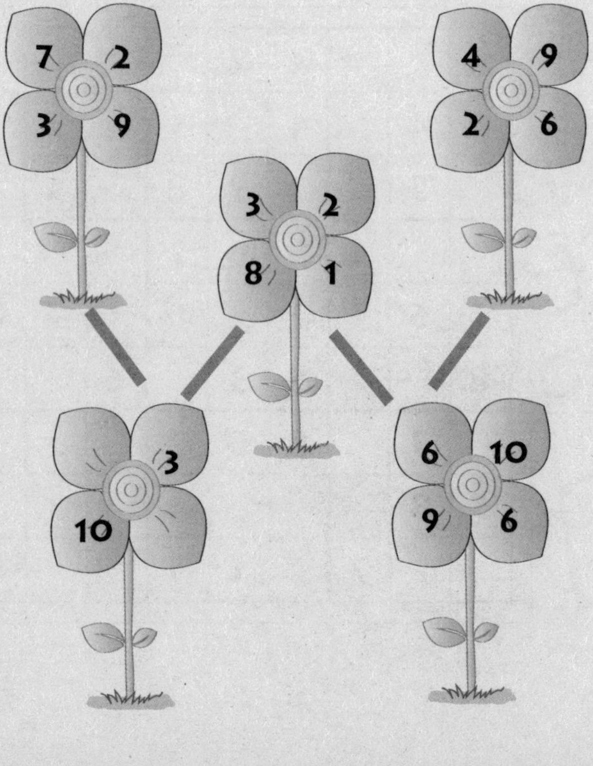

7 2
3 9

4 9
2 6

3 2
8 1

3
10

6 10
9 6

HONEYCOMB

Which number is the odd one out?

16

34

24

48

64

HOLE NUMBERS

Complete this puzzle by adding the correct number to the empty circle. (Clue: Straight thinking will not help you with this one!)

4	7	5
10		8
7	9	6

LEVEL 4

FIGURE-IT-OUT

Which four-figure answer is missing from the empty box?

SHAPE UP

Find the missing number to complete the puzzle.

	3	
8		4
	1	

	2	
9		4
	3	

	1	
8		6
	1	

	4	
9		
	1	

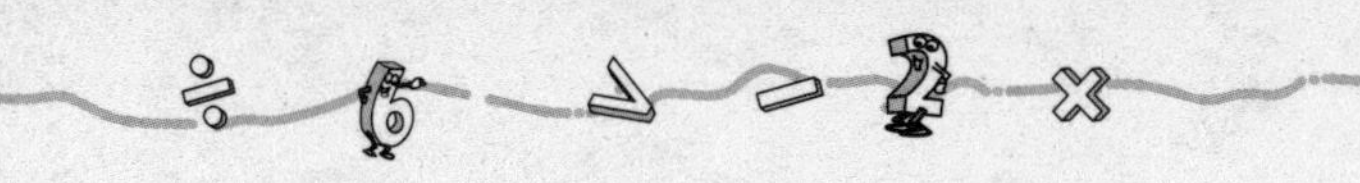

LEVEL 4

NUMBER WINDOW

Work out which number is missing and complete the puzzle.

4	8	1	6
2	1	2	8
5	5	2	4
3	1	?	2

GONE MISSING!

The number in the middle column has gone missing.
Can you replace it?
(Clue: Look at both sides of the grid.)

		12	6	2		
	6	7	8	3	2	
9	2	3	12	6	5	1
	4	8	14	11	7	
		13		9		

4 6 8 10 12 14

SUDOKU

2	4	3	6	9				
		7			4	9	8	3
	5			1	3			4
1	6			4		2		
	3	2	1		7	5	4	
		4		6			3	8
3			2	7			1	
4	9	6	8			3		
				3	9	8	6	5

NETWORK

Complete this puzzle by finishing off grids A and B, using the first grid as an example.

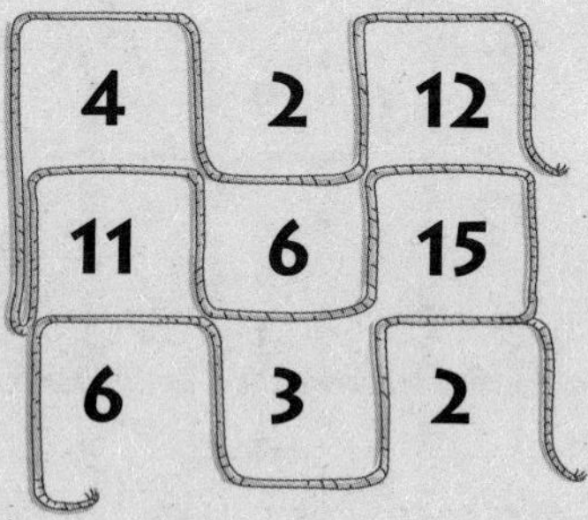

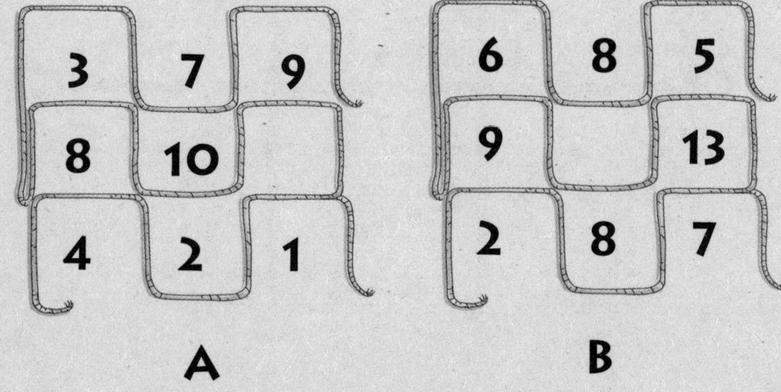

WHEEL SPIN

Which number is missing from the last wheel on the top row?
(Clue: The centre wheel in the top row is the link.)

SPACE ODDITY

Look at this little boy's glasses very carefully and work out which number is the odd one out in each oval.

TAKE AWAY

What number goes in the middle rectangle?
(Clue: It has got nothing to do with sums!)

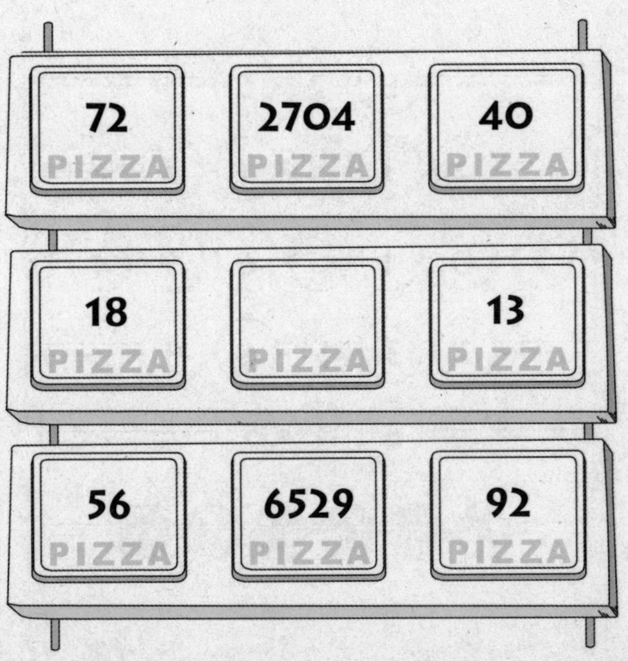

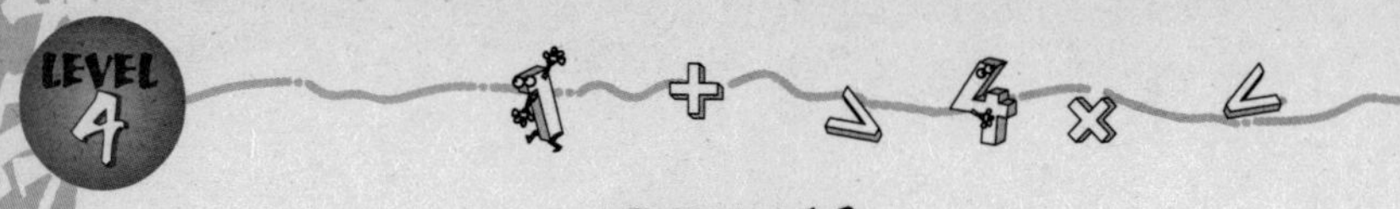

DOTTY!

Which of the bottom numbers will go into the centre dot?

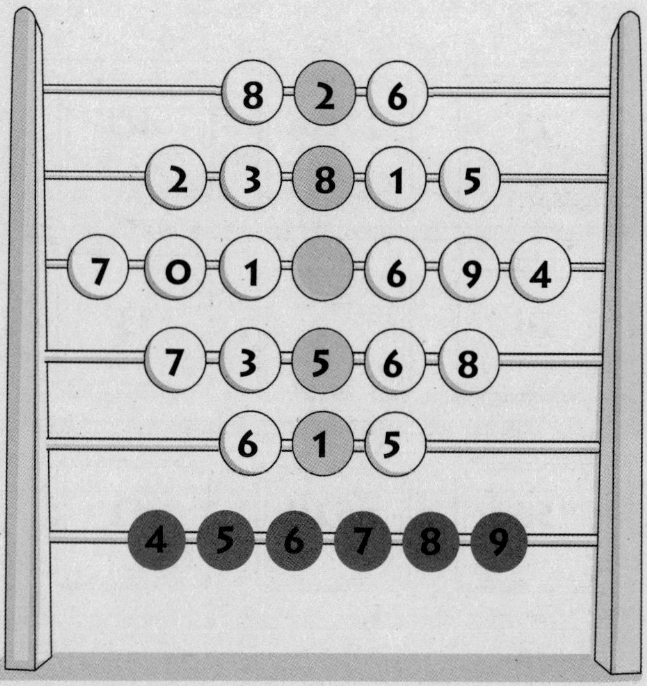

8 2 6

2 3 8 1 5

7 0 1 ◯ 6 9 4

7 3 5 6 8

6 1 5

4 5 6 7 8 9

ROGUE NUMBER

In each book we have added a rogue number.
Can you work out which one it is?

A

2 11 41 31 20

B

13 3 19 43 33

C

15 47 5 23 37

D

17 7 39 29 53

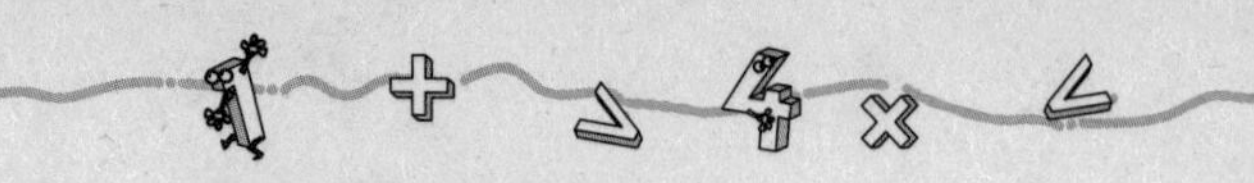

MISSING LINK

Which number completes this chain?

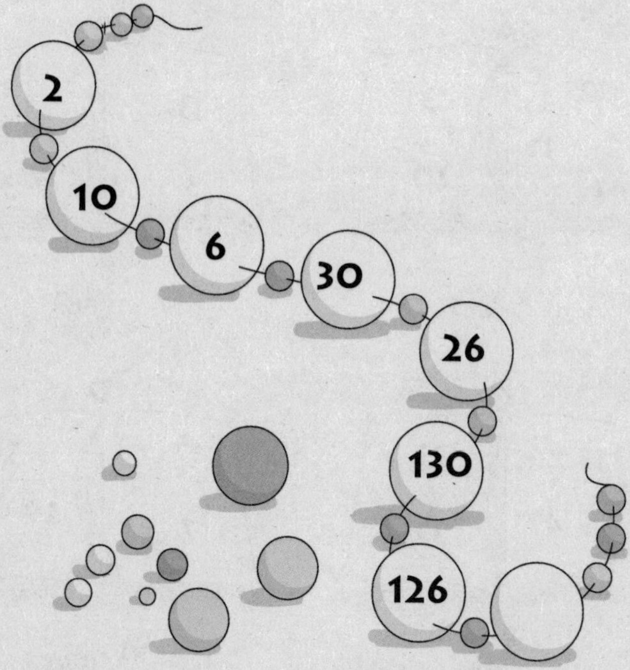

2

10

6

30

26

130

126

LEVEL 4

LINE UP

Using the same rule for every row, can you fill in the empty squares?

A	9	8	16	13	52	47
B	4	3	6		12	7
C	3	2		1	4	-1
D	7	6	12	9		31
E		4	8	5	20	15
F	8	7	14		44	39

LEVEL 4

SUDOKU

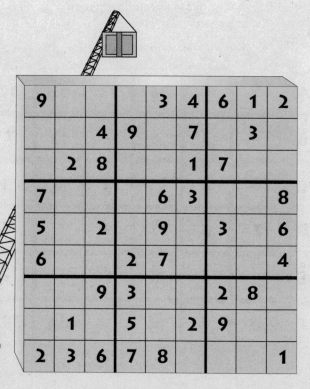

9				3	4	6	1	2
		4	9		7		3	
	2	8			1	7		
7				6	3			8
5		2		9		3		6
6			2	7				4
		9	3			2	8	
	1		5		2	9		
2	3	6	7	8				1

RING THE CHANGES

Which number goes in the empty ring?

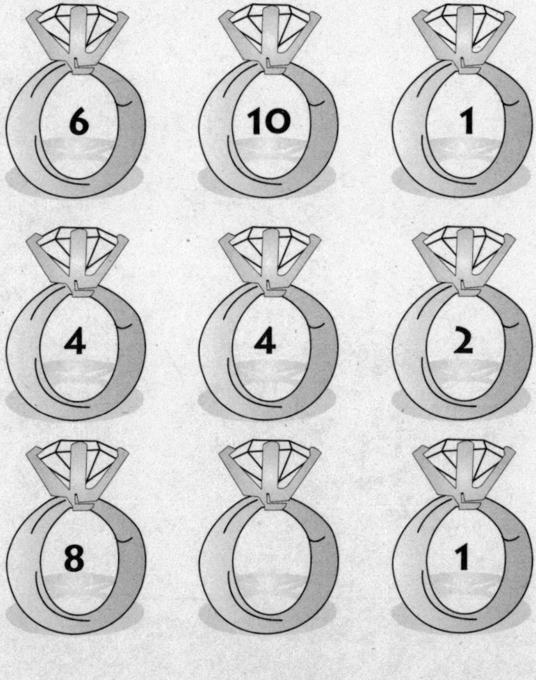

6	10	1
4	4	2
8		1

WHACKY WEB

Which number do you need to add in order to complete the web? (Clue: Find the link between each set of numbers.)

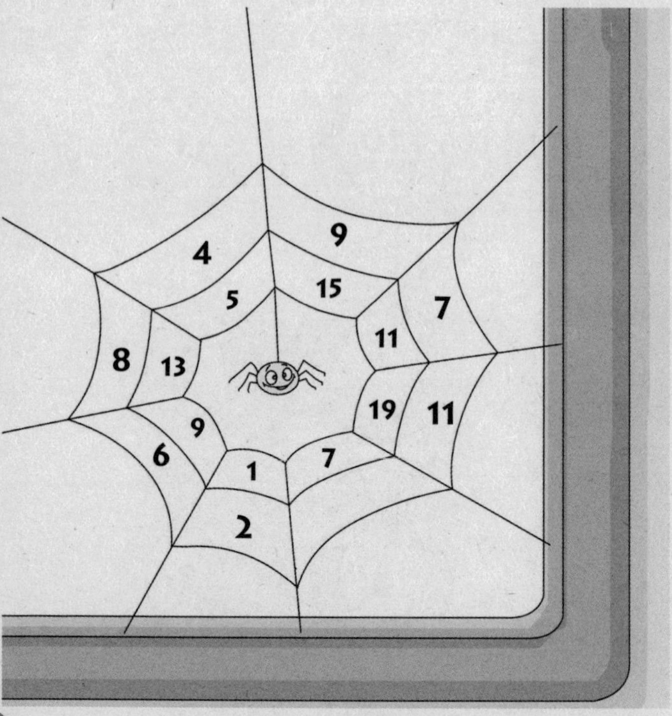

9
4
15
5
7
11
8
13
19
11
9
6
7
1
2

CHANGE IT

Replace the question mark with the correct number.
(Clue: Look at the numbers within each segment.)

LEVEL 4

OPTIONS

Which of the three numbers at the bottom will complete this puzzle? (Clue: Try looking up and down.)

NUMBER SQUARE

By using every number between 1 and 25 can you complete this number square so that every line, up and down, left to right and diagonal adds up to 65?

LEVEL 4

STAR STRUCK

Using the two completed stars as an example, work out what missing number is in the third.

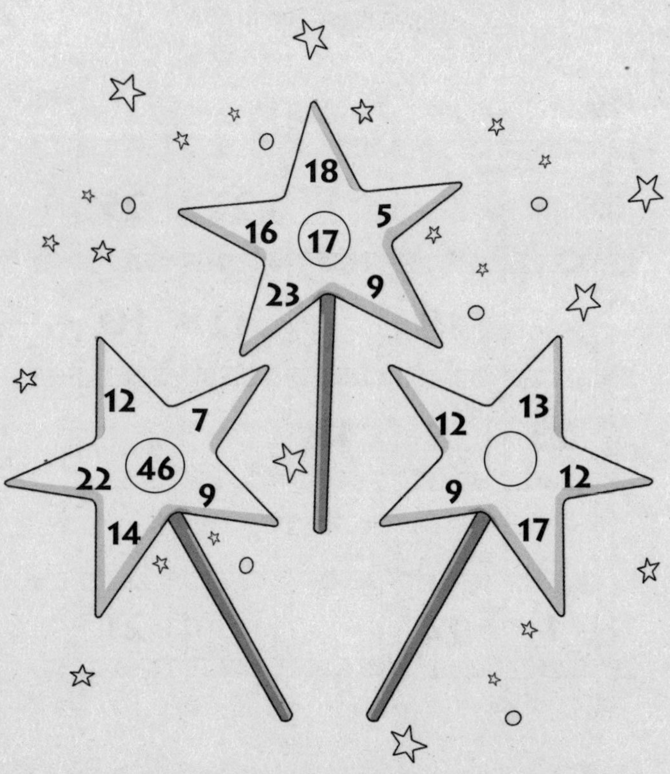

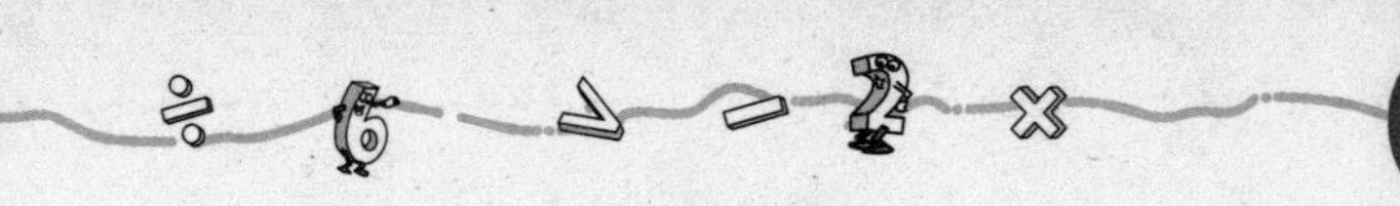

LEVEL 4

TRIO

Using the first two teddy bears as an example, fill in the empty space in the third.

GRID LOCK

Can you work out which numbers are required to complete grids A & B?

23	38	16
48	22	16
17	15	14

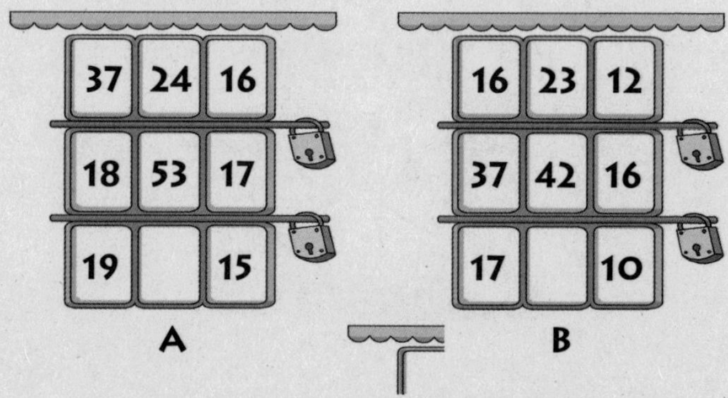

A

37	24	16
18	53	17
19		15

B

16	23	12
37	42	16
17		10

SUDOKU

	1		2	3				
	4	2			8	1		
	9			5		8	6	2
2		9	8		3	5		1
6	8			1			7	3
1		4	7		5	6		9
9	6	7		4			2	
		1	9			7	5	
				7	2		1	

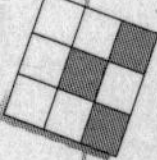

LINES OF THOUGHT

Put your thinking cap on and work out which number is missing from each line of octagons, use the first line as an example.

A	3	7	12	16	21	25
B	1	5		14	19	23
C		13	18	22	27	31
D	7	11	16		25	29
E	2		11	15	20	24
F	12	16	21	25		34

PYRAMID POINTERS

Which number goes on the top point of pyramid C?

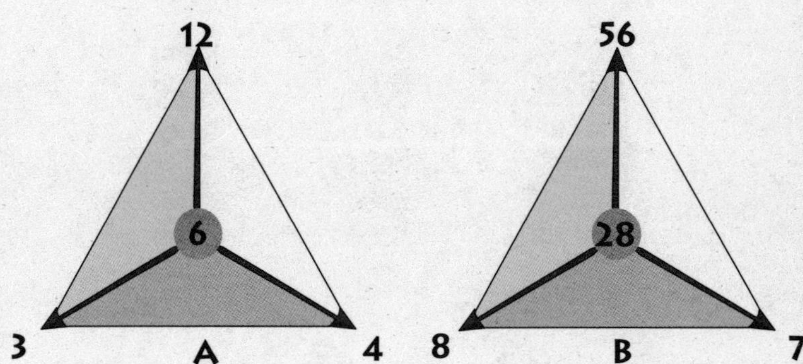

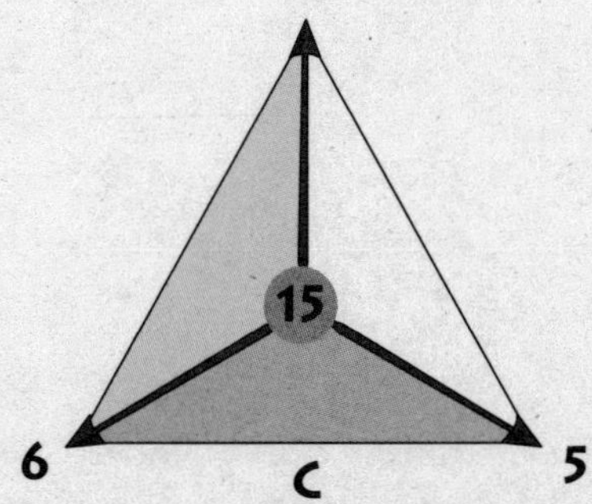

TIME OUT

What time should be shown on the blank watch at the end?

2 : 10

2 : 13

2 : 43

5 : 43

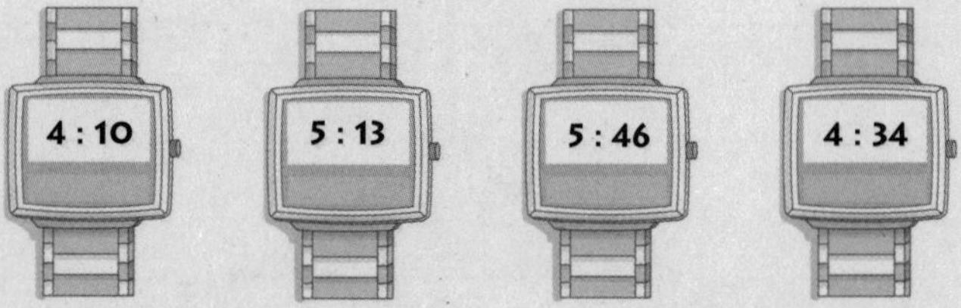

A	B	C	D
4 : 10	5 : 13	5 : 46	4 : 34

STAR STRUCK

Can you complete this puzzle by using the top two stars as a guide?

FIGURE-IT-OUT

Complete this puzzle by adding the correct number.
(Clue: Try looking at the puzzle from all directions.)

6	10	24
8	12	6
7	11	

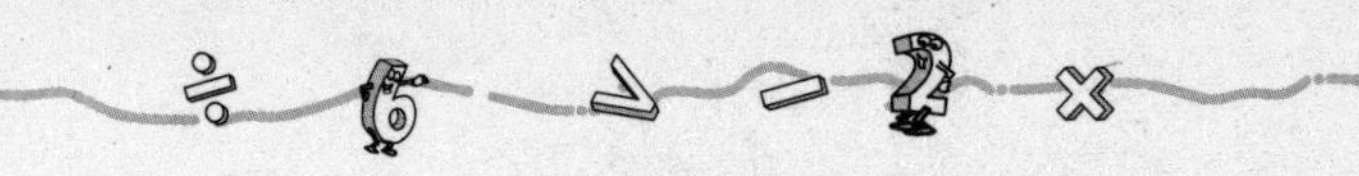

SLICED UP!

Can you work out which number is missing from the empty segment?
(Clue: Try stepping from one circle to another.)

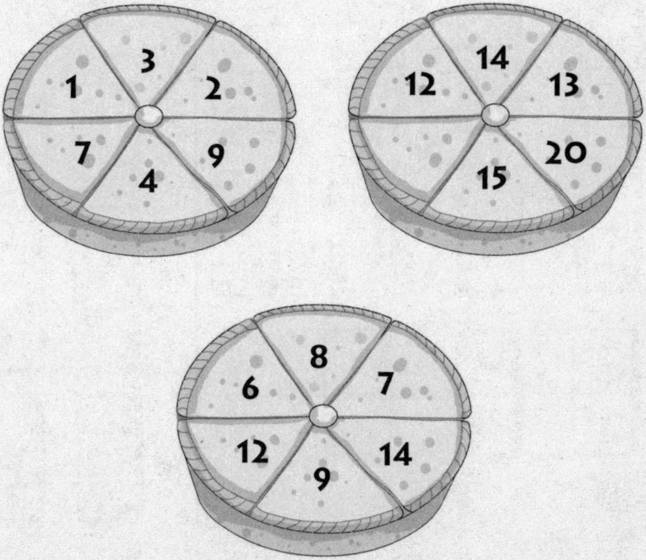

3
1 2
7 9
4

14
12 13
20
15

8
6 7
12 14
9

DOTTY DOMINOES!

Which of the six spare dominoes completes this dotty sequence?

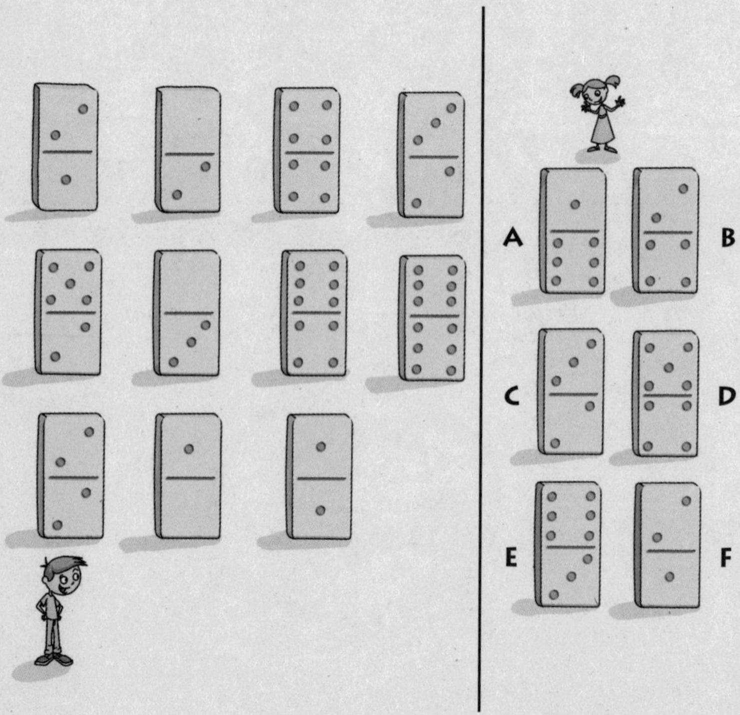

A

B

C

D

E

F

CIRCLES

Fill in the missing number.

ODD ONE OUT

Which number is the odd one out in each wheel?

CRAZY CLOCKS

Look carefully at the sequence of clocks and fill in the blank.

03:42

02:13

04:44

01:02

07:13

A

05:55

B

12:22

C

08:18

D

PYRAMID POSER

Work out which number goes at the top of the third pyramid.

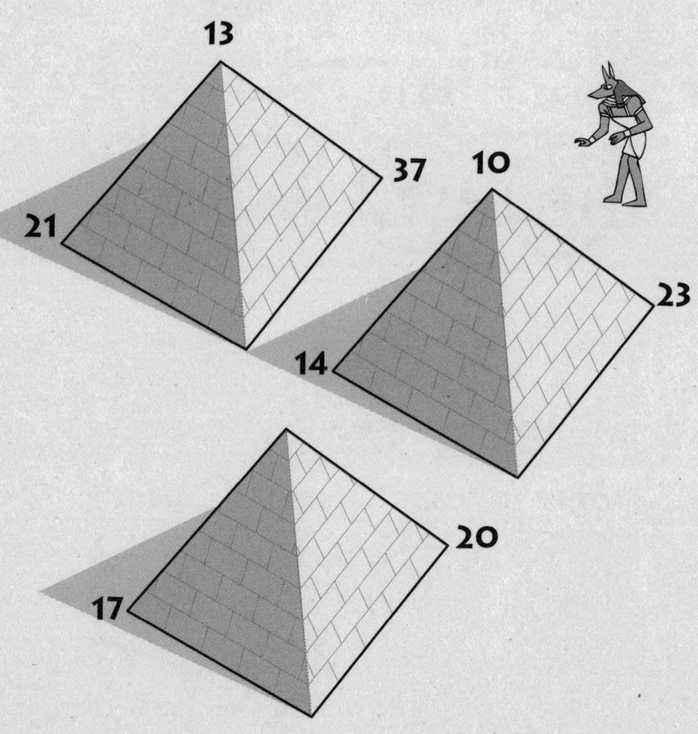

ALL SQUARE

Here is a complete puzzle - work out why it contains these numbers. (Clue: The centre square holds the answer.)

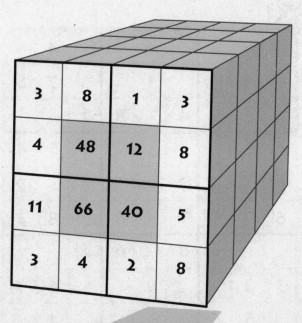

3	8	1	3
4	48	12	8
11	66	40	5
3	4	2	8

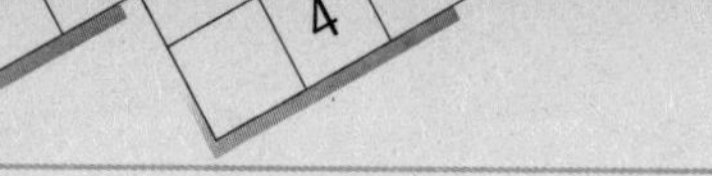

SUDOKU

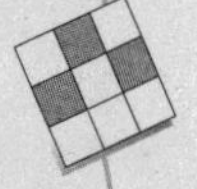

	8			6	2	3	4	
2	4			1			7	6
		3	4		8	2		
1	3		6		9		5	4
8		4	3		1	6		9
6	9		7		4		8	3
		7	8		6	5		
3	2			9			6	7
	5	6	2	3			1	

DOMINOES

By counting the dots on these dominoes, can you work out which of the six spare pieces completes the sequence?

CROSS OVER

Which number is missing from each puzzle?

TRI - PIE

Which number is missing from the empty segment?
(Clue: Look at the matching segments on each circle.)

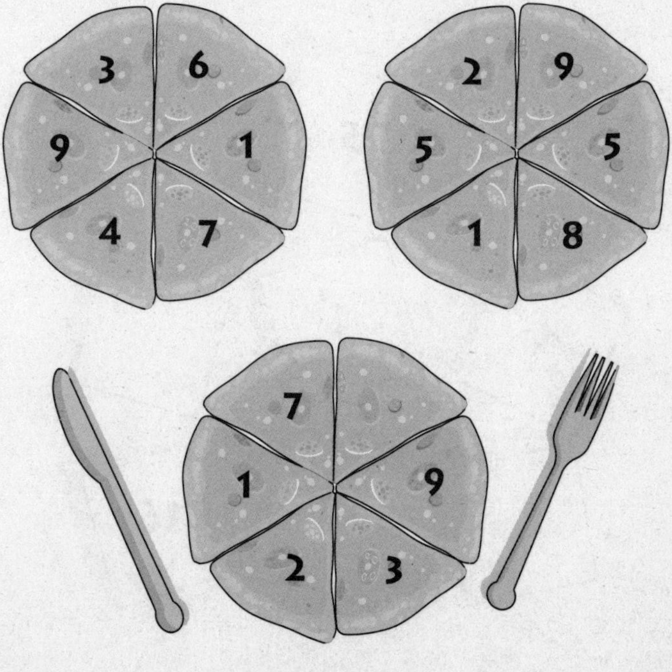

3 6
9 1
4 7

2 9
5 5
1 8

7
1 9
2 3

LEVEL 5

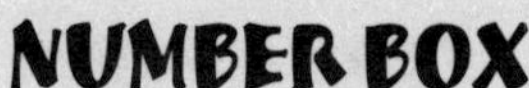

NUMBER BOX

Complete this number box by adding the correct number.
(Clue: The puzzle works up and down as well as side to side!)

3	5	9
4	1	
8	7	16

DIGITAL DISCS

Using the first two discs as an example, fill in the empty segment.

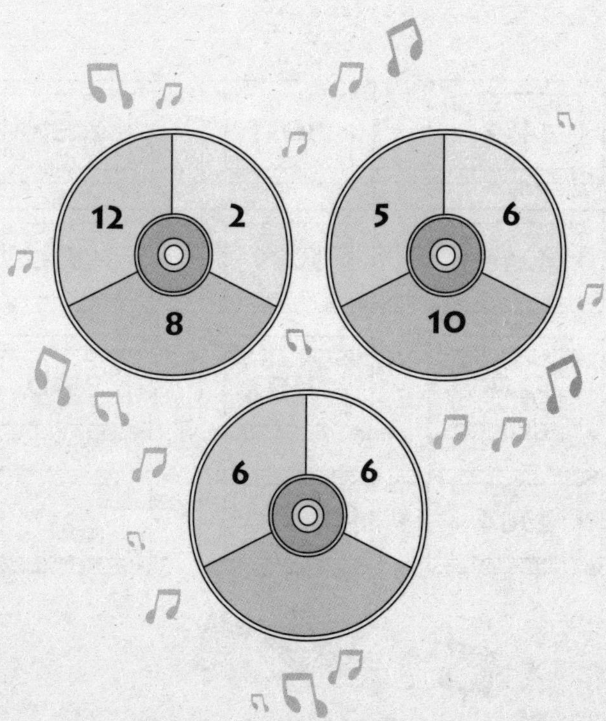

BOXING CLEVER

Can you work out which number is missing from the box on the bottom right? (Clue: Look at each row.)

CHOCOLATE 1452	CHOCOLATE 8031	CHOCOLATE 6132
CHOCOLATE 4216	CHOCOLATE 1039	CHOCOLATE 6520
CHOCOLATE 5216	CHOCOLATE 9503	CHOCOLATE 8510
CHOCOLATE 2364	CHOCOLATE 8070	CHOCOLATE 621?

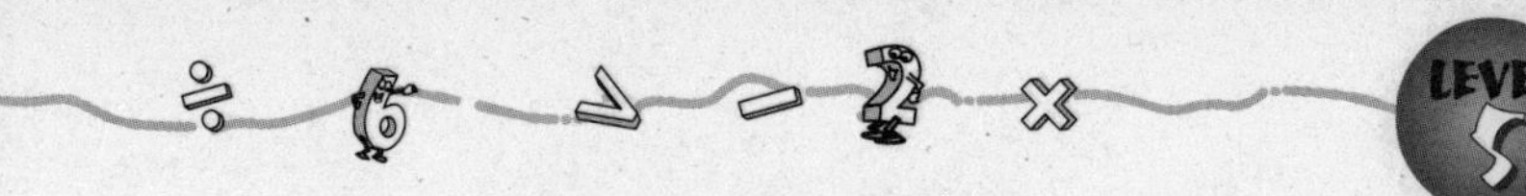

FOUR SQUARE

Fill in the empty shape and complete the puzzle.
(Clue: Look carefully at the different shading to find the pattern.)

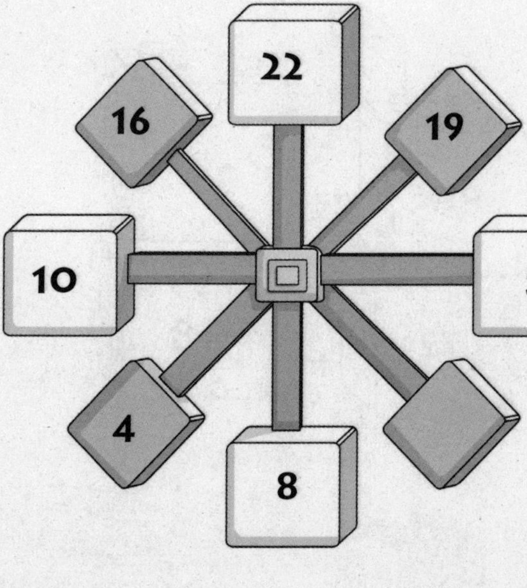

22

16

19

10

5

4

8

OUT OF PLACE

Which number doesn't go with the rest?

ET CETERA

Which number must be added to continue this sequence?

NUMBER WHEEL

Replace the question mark in this wheel with the correct number. (Clue: Don't just look at the numbers in the same segments.)

2 5
9 6
6 4
18 36
4 6 14 8
7 16 12 3
15 9
4 4
9 6
8 ?

SEQUENTIAL

Which number will complete this sequence?

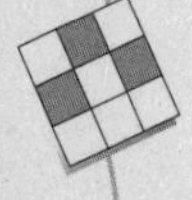

SUDOKU

		3	9			1	5	4
8	1			2		3		
6				3	5		7	2
3		4	2	7			8	
	7	8				6	3	8
	9			8	3	4		7
9	3		4	5				8
		2		1			9	6
1	5	7			6	2		

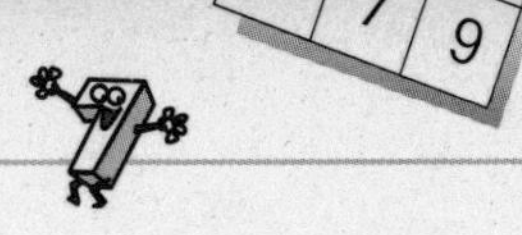

WEB WORLD

Which number replaces the question mark and completes the web?

	3	4	
	6	?	
2	3	2	9
8	1	9	6
	8	7	
	3	4	

MAGIC SQUARE

Fill in the empty space and complete the puzzle.
(Clue: Look carefully at the grid to find the pattern.)

9

1 2

2 36 1

3

2

ALL STAR

By using the first two stars as a guide, can you complete this puzzle?

CIRCLES

Which number is needed to finish the puzzle?

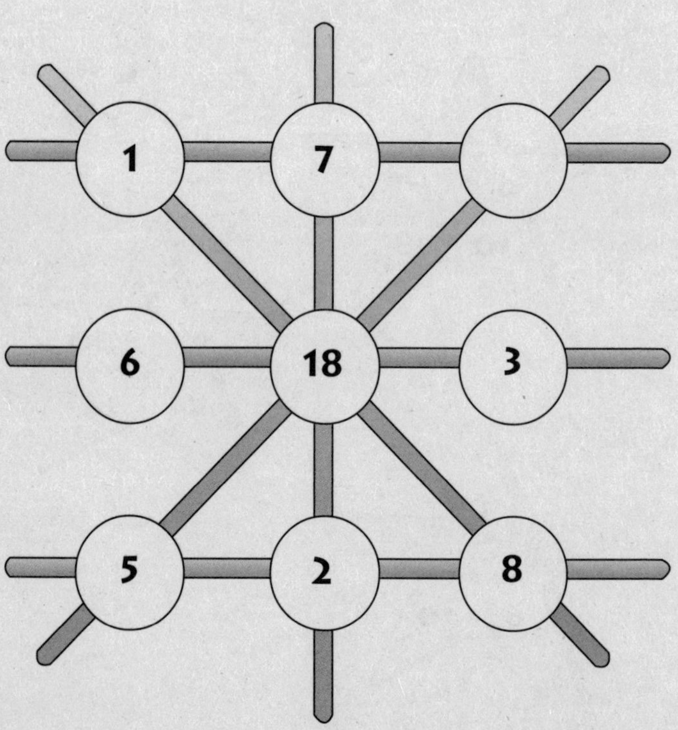

BOXING CLEVER

Which number completes this sequence?

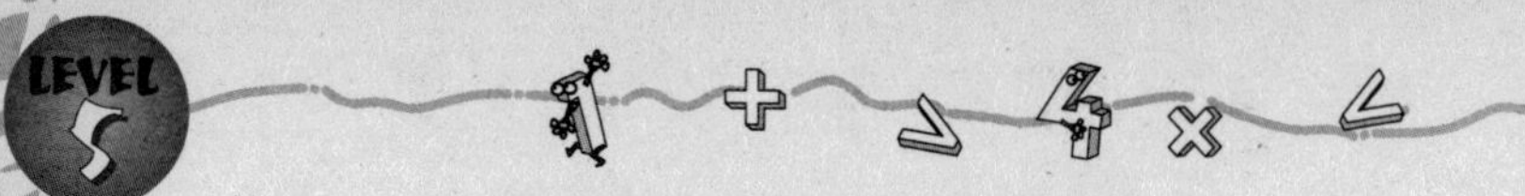

MISSING NUMBERS

Which numbers are missing from the empty petals?
(Clue: Look at the matching segments,
the middle flower is the link!)

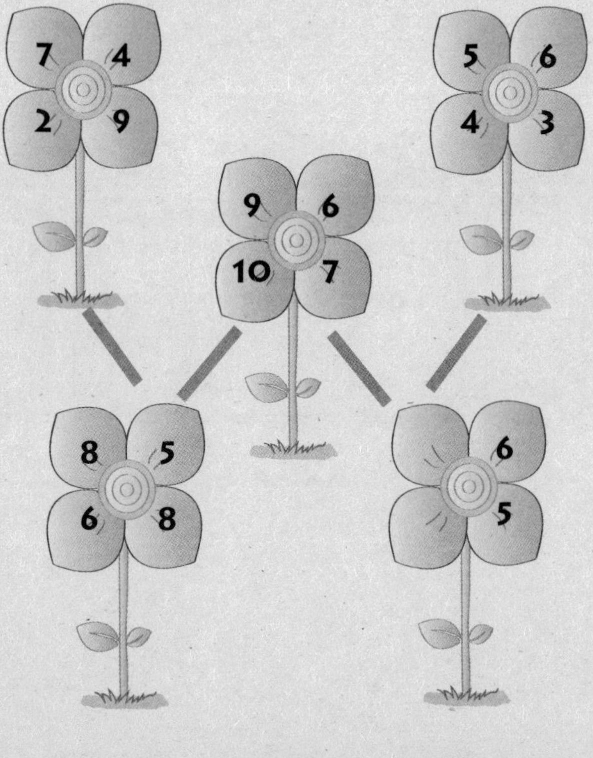

7 4
2 9

5 6
4 3

9 6
10 7

8 5
6 8

6
5

LEVEL 5

HONEYCOMB

Which number is the odd one out?

19

37

28

46

54

HOLE IN ONE

We have left a hole in this puzzle. Can you fill it with the correct number? (Clue: Don't think in straight lines.)

4	131	67
5		35
7	11	19

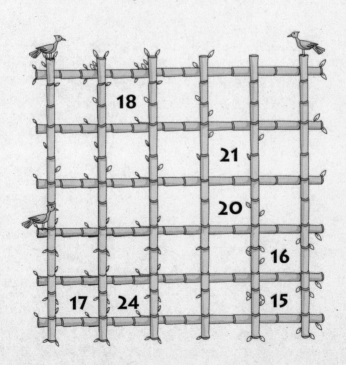

MAGIC SQUARE

By using every number between 1 and 25 can you complete this number square so that every line, up and down, left to right and diagonal adds up to 65?

	18			
			21	
			20	
				16
17	24			15

MISFITS

One number in each kite is a misfit - in other words it doesn't follow the same rules or requirements as all the others. Can you work out which one it is?

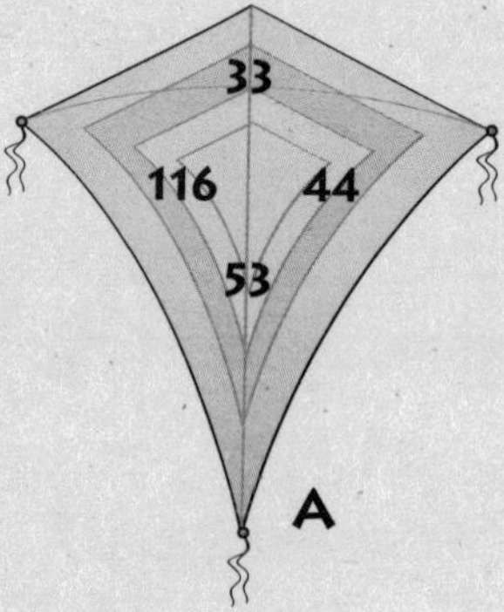

A: 33, 116, 44, 53

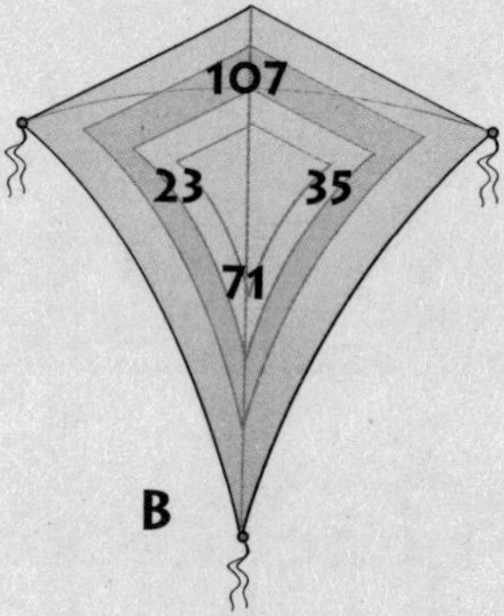

B: 107, 23, 35, 71

C: 16, 80, 134, 17

D: 34, 26, 62, 125

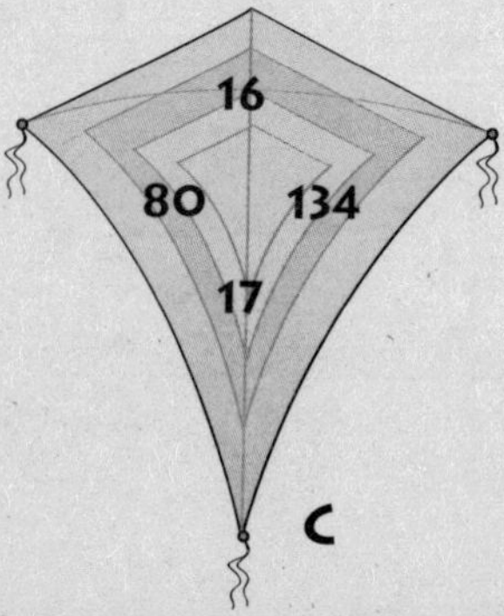

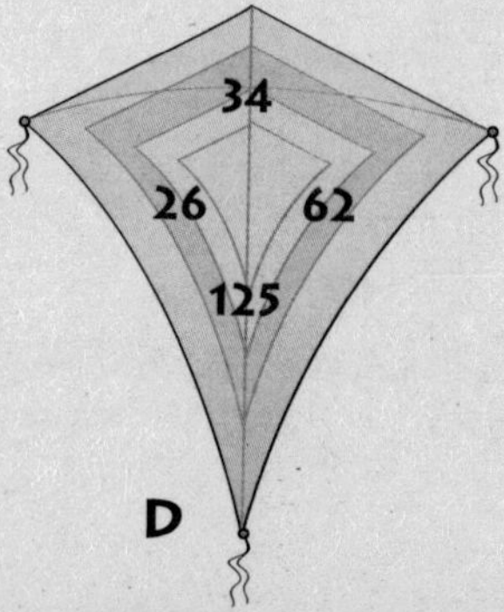

HOLE NUMBERS

Complete this puzzle by adding the correct number to the empty circle. (Clue: Straight thinking will not help you with this one!)

10	19	11
16		18
13	17	12

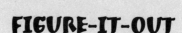

FIGURE-IT-OUT

Which four-figure answer is missing from the empty box?

6591	3648	1872
3248	2168	5364
7601	4169	2013
4824		3784

SHAPE UP

Find the missing number to complete the puzzle.

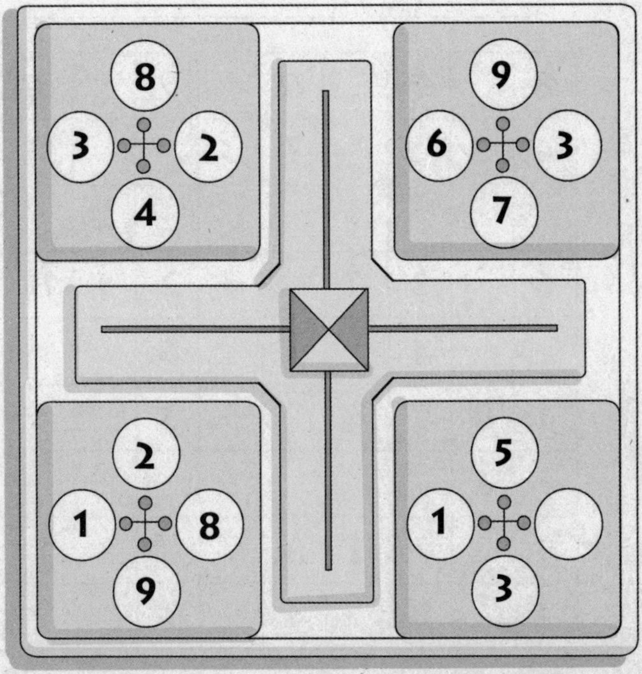

	Top	Left	Right	Bottom
Top left	8	3	2	4
Top right	9	6	3	7
Bottom left	2	1	8	9
Bottom right	5	1		3

SUDOKU

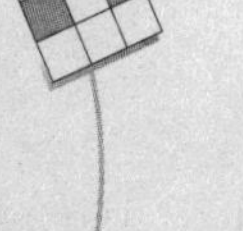

8		5		6		9		3
4	6			7	3			5
			1				2	
6		3	7		4	2	5	8
		4		3		6		
1	8	7	6		5	3		4
	7				6			
9			2	8			3	1
2		8		4		7		9

TAKE AWAY

What number goes in the middle rectangle?
(Clue: It has got nothing to do with sums!)

23 PIZZA	1832 PIZZA	81 PIZZA
74 PIZZA	PIZZA	67 PIZZA
92 PIZZA	5429 PIZZA	45 PIZZA

DOTTY!

Which of the bottom numbers will go into the centre dot?

7 7 3

6 2 8 8 5

3 4 2 ◯ 9 0 1

3 4 6 6 5

2 4 4

4 5 6 7 8 9

HOUSEY HOUSEY!

Using the first two houses as an example, can you work out which number is missing from the third house?

House	Roof	Top left	Top right	Bottom left	Door	Bottom right
1	3	29	11	24	8	28
2	6	16	10	15	6	13
3		20	8	17	6	

OPTIONAL EXTRAS

Which of the three optional extra numbers at the bottom will replace the question mark?
(Clue: Don't just look from left to right.)

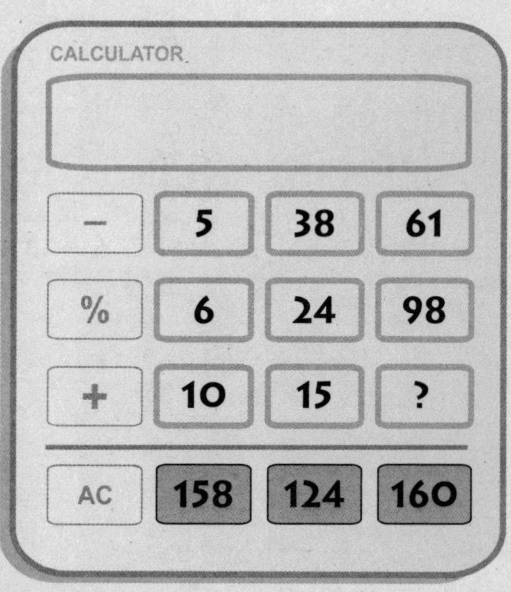

NUMBER SQUARE

This puzzle is a little bit different in that we have given you all the numbers already to show you what the finished teaser looks like. Can you work out why these numbers are correct?

(Clue: The centre square is the key.)

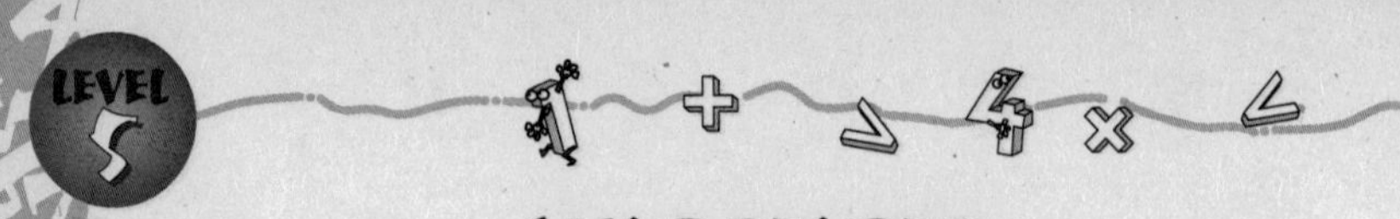

MIND BENDER

John, Paul, Peter and Andrew are all sharing their favourite sweets while watching their favourite TV programme. When the programme finishes, they realise that not everyone has had their fair share of sweets:

John owes **Paul** 1 sweet
Paul owes **Peter** 2 sweets
Peter owes **Andrew** 3 sweets
Andrew owes **John** 4 sweets

So that everyone gets the same number of sweets, what is the minimum number of sweets that have to be given to whom by who?

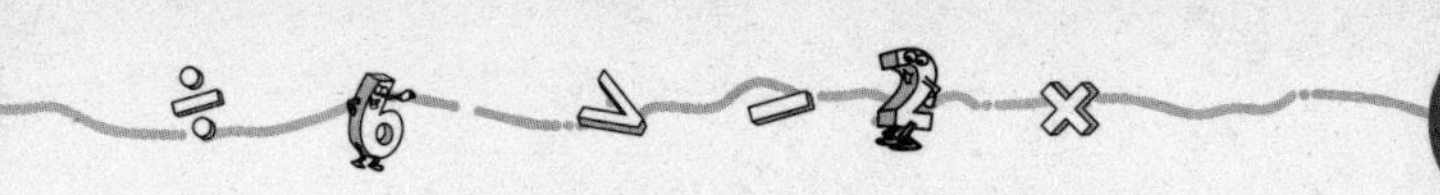

LEVEL 5

NUMBER WINDOW

Work out which number is missing and complete the puzzle.

0	2	3	6
2	1	4	6
9	14	6	10
8	16	?	11

GONE MISSING!

The number in the middle column has gone missing.
Can you replace it?
(Clue: Look at both sides of the grid.)

		2	5	8		
	5	9	13	17	21	
3	8	13	18	23	28	33
	1	7	13	19	25	
		4		18		

1 3 5 7 9 11

SUDOKU

2		8	1	4		9		3
7	6				3		8	5
9				7				6
	9	4	7	6	8			
5		2		9		1		8
			2	5	1	7	4	
6				3				4
3	2		4				5	1
4		5		1	9	3		7

ROGUE NUMBER

In each book we have added a rogue number.
Can you work out which one it is?

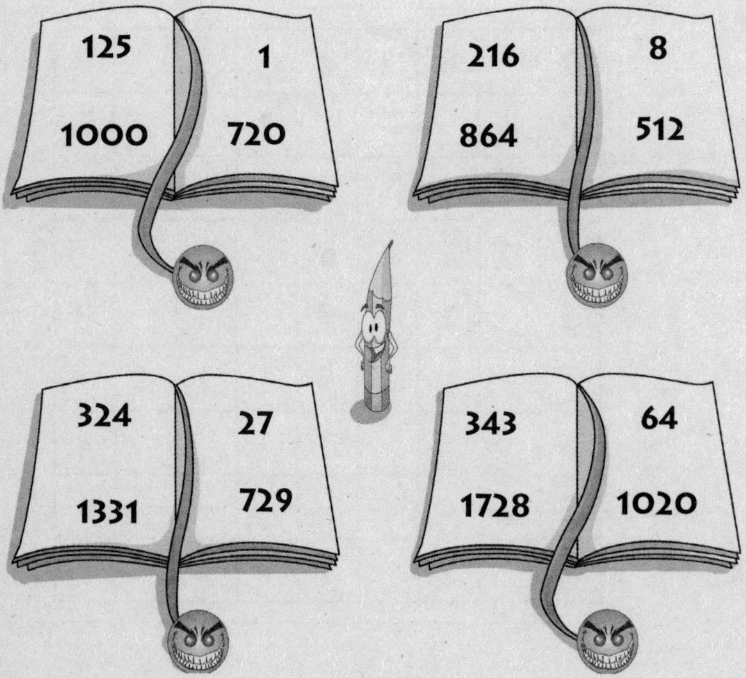

125 1
1000 720

216 8
864 512

324 27
1331 729

343 64
1728 1020

MISSING LINK

Which number completes this chain?

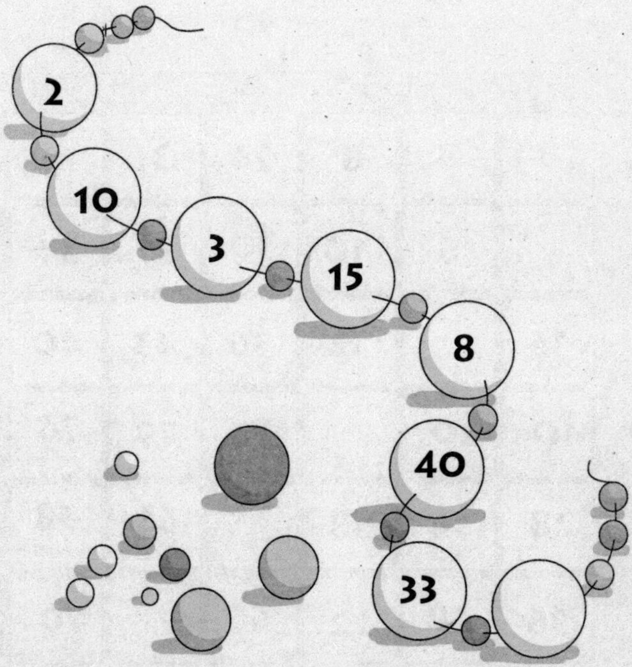

2 10 3 15 8 40 33

LEVEL 5

LINE UP

Using the same rule for every row, can you fill in the empty squares.

A	8	4	8	24	31	
B		6	10	30	37	34
C	16		12	36	43	40
D	40	20		72	79	76
E	28	14	18		61	58
F	36	18	22	66		70

CHANGE IT

Replace the question mark with the correct number.
(Clue: Look at the numbers within each segment.)

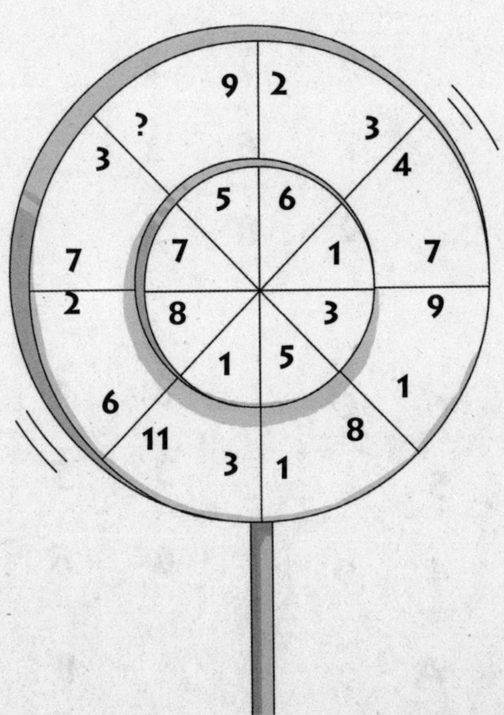

NETWORK

Complete this puzzle by finishing off grids A and B, using the first grid as an example.

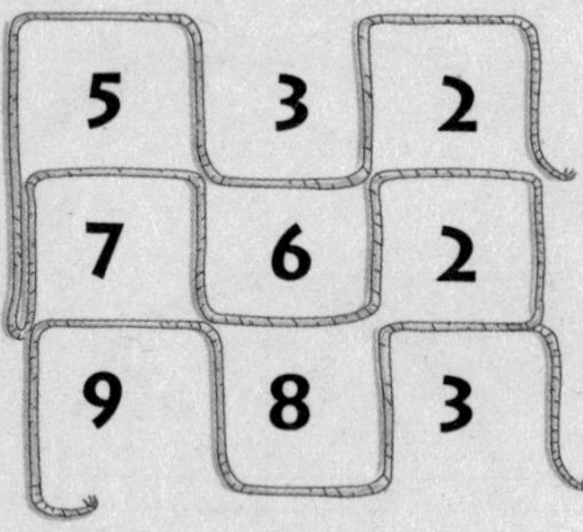

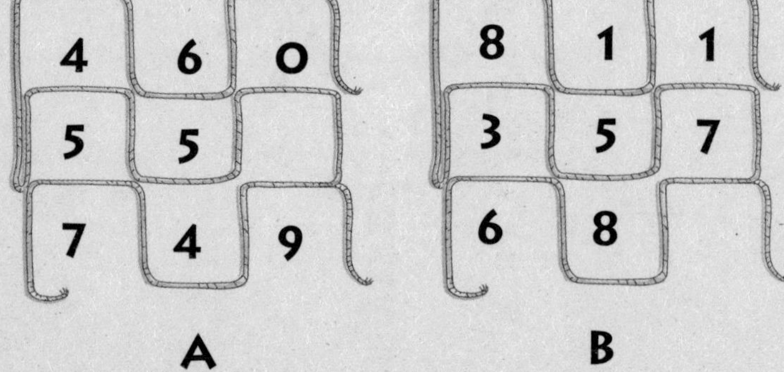

WHEEL SPIN

Which numbers are missing from the empty wheel?

Wheel	Top left	Top right	Bottom left	Bottom right
Top left wheel	1	3	6	2
Top middle wheel	6	8	11	7
Top right wheel (empty)				
Bottom left wheel	3	5	8	4
Bottom right wheel	10	12	15	11

SPACE ODDITY

Look at this little boy's glasses very carefully and work out which number is the odd one out in each oval.

A

9

64

25

72

49

B

109

216

8

125

1

7. LINES OF THOUGHT

Line B = 12
Line C = 10
Line D = 8
Line E = 4
Line F = 24
As you move from left to right, add 2 to the first number, then 3, then 4 etc.

8. PYRAMID POINTERS

Answer = 5
In each triangle, add the lower two numbers together to give the number at the top of the triangle.

9. TIME OUT

Answer = C
Start with the watch on the left and move to the right. The time on each watch increases by 1 hour and 10 minutes each time.

10. STAR STRUCK

Answer = 12
Start with the number at the top of each star, and move clockwise around the star's points. The numbers increase by this top number each time, as you go round.

11. FIGURE-IT-OUT

Answer = 8
In each row and column, add together the left and right hand numbers, or the top and bottom numbers, to get the result in the centre of the row or column.

12. SLICED UP

Answer = 16
One way of doing this is to divide each circle in half, vertically. In each half, multiply the top number by the middle number to give the lower number.

13. SUDOKU

1	9	8	5	3	7	6	2	4
5	3	6	8	4	2	9	1	7
4	2	7	1	6	9	5	3	8
8	1	4	7	2	5	3	6	9
6	7	2	3	9	4	1	8	5
9	5	3	6	1	8	7	4	2
7	4	1	2	5	6	8	9	3
2	6	5	9	8	3	4	7	1
3	8	9	4	7	1	2	5	6

14. ODD ONE OUT

Wheel A = 2
It is the only even number.
Wheel B = 15
It is the only odd number.

15. CRAZY CLOCKS

Answer = C
The time increases by 1 hour and 5 minutes each step.

16. PYRAMID POSER

Answer = 12
Add the bottom two numbers together to get the top number.

3 + 7 = 10
6 + 3 = 9
8 + 4 = 12

17. ALL SQUARE

Add the three outer numbers and write the answer in the inner corner.

18. DOTTY DOMINOES

Answer = A
Start at the top left, and work in rows, from left to right, top to bottom.
The spot total on each domino follows the sequence 1, 2, 3, 4... etc.

Top	Bottom	Total
1		=1
	2	=2
1	2	=3
4		=4
3	2	=5
6		=6
5	2	=7
6	2	=8
3	6	=9
5	5	=10
6	5	=11
6	6	=12

19. CIRCLES

Answer = 9

Work through the diagram in rows. Add the left hand number to the central number, to get the result in the right hand circle.

20. SUDOKU

2	1	7	3	9	6	8	4	5
8	3	9	5	4	7	2	6	1
5	6	4	2	8	1	3	7	9
6	8	3	4	1	2	9	5	7
4	7	5	8	6	9	1	2	3
9	2	1	7	3	5	4	8	6
7	9	2	1	5	8	6	3	4
1	4	8	6	7	3	5	9	2
3	5	6	9	2	4	7	1	8

21. DIGITAL DISCS

Answer = 51

Multiply the top two numbers and write the answer, in reverse, in the bottom segment.

22. BOXING CLEVER

Answer = 9

Read each row as a 3 digit number. Starting at the top and working down, numbers are written in sequence, starting at 100, then 121, 144 and 169. These numbers represent the square numbers of 10, 11, 12 and 13.

23. FOUR SQUARE

Answer = 1

There are 2 groups of 4 circles in the diagram, each one defining a square. The sum of the numbers in each square is 14.

24. OUT OF PLACE

Answer = 10

All the other numbers are multiples of 3.

25. ET CETERA

Answer = 128

Numbers double each step.

26. SUDOKU

1	6	4	9	2	3	8	5	7
5	2	9	7	8	6	4	1	3
7	8	3	4	5	1	9	2	6
2	9	1	3	4	5	6	7	8
4	3	5	8	6	7	1	9	2
8	7	6	2	1	9	5	3	4
6	1	2	5	7	8	3	4	9
9	5	7	6	3	4	2	8	1
3	4	8	1	9	2	7	6	5

27. DOMINOES

Answer = D

The dots on the dominoes in the last column equal the total of all the other dots in the same row.

2 / -	4 / 3	- / 1	=	6 / 4
1 / 3	2 / 1	1 / 1	=	4 / 5
- / 3	4 / -	2 / 2	=	6 / 5

28. CROSS OVER

The middle number in each case is made up of the outer numbers, so that:

A = 2 4 + 7 + 1 + 2 = 14
B = 2 5 + 1 + 3 + 2 = 11
C = 6 1 + 8 + 2 + 6 = 17

29. TRI-PIE

Answer = 18

Moving clockwise around each circle, starting with the lowest number, the numbers increase by 1, then 2, then 3, etc.

30. NUMBER BOX

Answer = 1

Add together the first and second numbers in each line to get the third.

3 + 4 = 7
2 + 1 = 3
5 + 5 = 10

31. WEB WORLD

Answer = 5

The numbers in the inner ring have been moved one place clockwise from the numbers in the outer ring.

32. MAGIC SQUARE

Answer = 15

The four numbers at the corners of the square when added together = 15, and the four numbers which make up the diamond when added together = 15.

33. ALL STAR

Answer = 5

In each star the top number will divide into the other numbers.

34. CIRCLES

Answer = 9

Add together the numbers on the end of each line to get the middle number.

35. SUDOKU

1	6	4	7	9	8	2	5	3
9	3	8	6	2	5	1	4	7
5	7	2	1	4	3	8	9	6
7	4	9	5	1	6	3	8	2
8	2	1	4	3	7	9	6	5
6	5	3	2	8	9	4	7	1
4	8	6	3	5	1	7	2	9
3	9	7	8	6	2	5	1	4
2	1	5	9	7	4	6	3	8

36. NUMBER WHEEL

Answer = 1

Add up the 2 numbers in each segment, and add this total to the sum of the numbers in the opposite segment. This always makes 10.

37. SEQUENTIAL

Answer = 32

As you move from left to right, double the previous number to get the next one along.

38. HOLE IN ONE

Answer = 20

Start with the 4 in the top left of the puzzle, and move in a clockwise spiral direction towards the centre. The numbers follow the sequence of multiples of 4, from 4 to 36.

39. MAGIC SQUARE

9	4	5
2	6	10
7	8	3

40. MISFITS

A = 21 all numbers are multiples of 5

B = 41 all numbers are multiples of 6

C = 10 all numbers are multiples of 3

D = 15 all numbers are multiples of 4

41. HOUSEY HOUSEY

Answer = 16

The number on the roof of each house equals the sum of the numbers in the windows and doors.

42. OPTIONAL EXTRAS

Answer = 12

In each column, add the top number to the middle number to give the result on the bottom row.

43. BOXING CLEVER

Answer = 17

Double each number and subtract 1 to get the next.

44. MISSING NUMBERS

Answer = 9 and 9

The numbers in each of the segments in the bottom flowers are equal to the sum of the corresponding segments in the connected

flowers above.
Left and centre flowers:
2 + 7 = 9
4 + 1 = 5
3 + 2 = 5
1 + 5 = 6
Centre and right flowers:
7 + 2 = 9
1 + 3 = 4
2 + 4 = 6
5 + 4 = 9

45. SUDOKU

1	3	5	4	6	9	2	7	8
4	8	9	3	7	2	5	1	6
7	6	2	5	1	8	4	3	9
6	9	7	2	5	4	1	8	3
2	4	8	1	9	3	7	6	5
3	5	1	6	8	7	9	2	4
8	1	3	9	2	5	6	4	7
5	7	6	8	4	1	3	9	2
9	2	4	7	3	6	8	5	1

46. HONEYCOMB
Answer = 22
All the other numbers are odd.

47. HOLE NUMBERS
Answer = 37
Starting in the top left corner and moving clockwise in a spiral pattern towards the centre, add 1, then 2, then 3 etc.

48. FIGURE-IT-OUT
Answer = 989
Add the numbers in the two out of boxes of each column together to get the middle one.

49. SHAPE UP
Answer = 2
Add together each pair of opposite numbers to get the same total.

50. TAKE AWAY
Answer = 3734
Put the two digits from the right hand side in the middle of the two digits from the left hand side.

51. DOTTY

Answer = 6

Add together the numbers on the left-hand side of the shaded column, then add together the numbers on the right and the difference is shown in the centre.

52. SUDOKU

2	5	3	1	8	7	4	9	6
6	1	7	4	9	2	8	3	5
8	9	4	6	3	5	7	2	1
1	8	6	7	5	9	3	4	2
7	3	5	2	4	6	1	8	9
4	2	9	3	1	8	5	6	7
5	6	1	8	2	3	9	7	4
3	4	2	9	7	1	6	5	8
9	7	8	5	6	4	2	1	3

53. NUMBER SQUARE

If you add up the 3 numbers in each outer square, the total is always 10.

54. MINDBENDER

£20 profit. On each deal he made a £10 profit.

55. NUMBER WINDOW

Answer = 0

Read the 2 separate digits in each box as a whole 2 digit number. Moving from left to right, top row then bottom, the 2 digit numbers increase by 5 each time, from 25 to 40.

56. GONE MISSING

Answer = 3

In each row, add up the numbers to the left of the centre, and subtract the numbers to the right of the centre, putting the result in the dark circle in the centre.

57. NETWORK

Answer A = 1 and B = 5

Add the top number to the bottom number of every

column to get the same answer for each column.

58. WHEEL SPIN

Answer = 7

Add together the numbers in the matching segments of the upper left and middle circles, putting the results in the same segments of the lower left circle. Repeat the same process for the middle and upper right circles.

59. SUDOKU

5	1	8	7	9	6	2	4	3
7	6	4	8	3	2	9	1	5
9	3	2	4	5	1	7	6	8
4	9	6	1	7	5	3	8	2
1	7	5	2	8	3	6	9	4
2	8	3	9	6	4	5	7	1
8	2	9	5	1	7	4	3	6
3	5	7	6	4	8	1	2	9
6	4	1	3	2	9	8	5	7

60. SPACE ODDITY

Oval A = 6

All the numbers are odd.

Oval B = 7

All the numbers are even.

61. RING THE CHANGES

Answer = 5

In each row of the diagram, subtract the right hand number from the left hand number to give the result in the middle ring.

62. WHACKY WEB

Answer = 4

Add together pairs of numbers, one from an outer segment and one from the inner segment directly opposite. Their total should always be 10.

63. ROGUE NUMBER

A = 11 The only odd number

B = 13 The only odd number

C = 12 The only even number
D = 16 The only even number

64. MISSING LINK
Answer = 38
Moving from left to right, add 2, then 3, then 4 etc.

65. LINE UP
Line B = 13
Line C = 5
Line D = 6
Line E = 9
Line F = 8
Moving along the rows, add three and then subtract 1 and continue this sequence until the end.

66. CHANGE IT
Answer = 18
The number in the centre is mid-way between the outer two numbers in each segment.

67. OPTIONS
Answer = 15
Moving down the first column, up the second and down the third, add three each step.

68. NUMBER SQUARE
Numbers in each row add up to 18

5	10	3
4	6	8
9	2	7

69. SUDOKU

9	5	1	4	8	3	6	7	2
2	3	7	6	9	1	5	4	8
8	6	4	7	2	5	1	3	9
6	2	9	5	7	4	8	1	3
1	7	5	3	6	8	2	9	4
4	8	3	9	1	2	7	5	6
7	4	6	2	5	9	3	8	1
5	9	8	1	3	6	4	2	7
3	1	2	8	4	7	9	6	5

70. STAR STRUCK

Answer = 12

Add up the outer numbers and divide the answer by 2 to get the middle number.

71. TRIO

Answer = 48

Multiply the top two numbers and double it to get the bottom number.

72. GRID LOCK

Answer: A = 1 and B = 8

Taking each box individually, the sum of the digits in each column are the same in each box.

73. LINES OF THOUGHT

Line B = 1
Line C = 4
Line D = 13
Line E = 9
Line F = 6
In each row, add the first two numbers together and add 2 to give the next number along.

74. PYRAMID POINTERS

Answer = 6
In each triangle, add together the bottom 2 numbers and subtract 2 to give the value at the top of the triangle.

75. TIME OUT

Answer = A
Starting with the watch on the left and moving to the right, the time on each watch increases by 50 minutes.

76. STAR STRUCK

Answer = 7
In each star, start at the top point and move clockwise. Add the first two numbers together to give the next one along. Continue this pattern all the way around each star.

77. FIGURE-IT-OUT

Answer = 2
The numbers create a magic square, in which the numbers along any vertical, horizontal or diagonal line add up to 15.

78. SUDOKU

3	8	4	9	1	2	7	6	5
7	1	9	6	4	5	2	3	8
2	5	6	8	3	7	1	4	9
4	9	2	5	7	8	6	1	3
6	7	1	2	9	3	8	5	4
5	3	8	4	6	1	9	2	7
8	6	7	3	2	4	5	9	1
1	2	3	7	5	9	4	8	6
9	4	5	1	8	6	3	7	2

79. SLICED UP

Answer = 8

Add together numbers in matching segments of the upper left and right hand circles, and put the result in the matching segments of the lower circle.

80. DOTTY DOMINOES

Answer = C

In each row, starting on the left and moving to the right, the spot total on each domino increases by 2 each time.

1/1	3/1	2/4	6/2
1/	2/1	3/2	1/6
2/2	3/3	6/2	= 5/5

81. CIRCLES

Answer = 8

Work through the diagram in columns. If you multiply the top number by the middle number you get the result, shown by the bottom number.

82. DIGITAL DISCS

Answer = 37

In each circle, multiply the left and right hand numbers together and subtract 3 to give the lower number.

83. BOXING CLEVER

Answer = 279

In each row of the diagram, add the number in the left hand column to the number in the right hand column and put the result in the central column.

84. ODD ONE OUT

Wheel A = 10

It is the only number not divisible by 3.

Wheel B = 25
It is the only number not divisible by 7.

85. CRAZY CLOCKS

Answer = B
The time decreases by 1 hour and 12 minutes each step.

86. PYRAMID POSER

Answer = 14
Multiply the bottom two numbers together to get the top number.
4 x 5 = 20
3 x 6 = 18
2 x 7 = 14

87. ALL SQUARE

The outer numbers are all divisible by the inner number.

88. SUDOKU

9	1	6	3	2	8	7	5	4
7	5	4	6	9	1	8	2	3
2	8	3	7	4	5	9	6	1
1	7	5	2	6	9	3	4	8
4	9	8	5	7	3	6	1	2
3	6	2	1	8	4	5	7	9
8	2	7	4	3	6	1	9	5
5	4	9	8	1	7	2	3	6
6	3	1	9	5	2	4	8	7

89. DOMINOES

Answer = A
The total number of dots on each domino increases by 2 each step of the line.

3/1	-/6	5/3	5/5	
1/-	-/3	1/4	6/1	
1/2	2/3	4/3	=	4/5

90. CROSS OVER

Add together the numbers at each end of the diagonal lines to get the middle number.

A = 13 7 + 6 = 13 9 + 4 = 13
B = 9 2 + 9 = 11 6 + 5 = 11
C = 2 1 + 7 = 8 2 + 6 = 8

91. TRI-PIE

Answer = 7

Add together the matching segments from the two circles on the right and transfer the answer to the corresponding segment in the third circle.

92. NUMBER BOX

Answer = 6

Multiply together the first and second numbers in each line to get the third.

2 x 3 = 6
3 x 1 = 3
6 x 3 = 18

93. BOXING CLEVER

Answer = 217

In each row of the diagram, add the number in the left hand column to the number in the right hand column and put the result in the central column.

94. FOUR SQUARE

Answer = 9

Look at the diagram as 2 interlocked squares. Starting with the lowest number in each square, move clockwise around the other numbers. One square contains the sequence of multiples of 2 (2, 4, 6, 8) and the other square contains multiples of 3 (3, 6, 9, 12).

95. OUT OF PLACE

Answer = 44

All the other numbers in the row are square numbers.

96. ET CETERA

Answer = 88

Start on the left and move to the right. Add the first 2 numbers together and add a further 1 to give the next number along.

97. WEB WORLD

Answer = 3

The numbers in the inner ring have been moved one place clockwise from the numbers in the outer ring with 1 then subtracted.

98. MAGIC SQUARE

Answer = 3

The four numbers at the corners of the square when added together = 23, and the four numbers which make up the diamond when added together also = 23.

99. ALL STAR

Answer = 12

Starting with the top number and moving clockwise add 1 to get the next number, then 2, then 3 etc.

100. RING THE CHANGES

Answer = 15

Add together the left and right-hand numbers, as well as multiplying them (5+8 and 5x8) Add these two answers together to get the middle number.

101. SUDOKU

1	2	3	8	9	6	7	4	5
9	5	6	4	2	7	3	1	8
8	7	4	3	1	5	6	9	2
6	4	7	2	5	9	1	8	3
2	3	9	1	7	8	5	6	4
5	8	1	6	3	4	9	2	7
4	9	2	7	6	3	8	5	1
3	1	5	9	8	2	4	7	6
7	6	8	5	4	1	2	3	9

102. NUMBER WHEEL

Answer = 5

In each segment, add the outer 2 numbers together, then add a further 1 to give the result at the centre of the segment.

103. SEQUENTIAL

Answer = 11

As you move from left to right, the numbers follow the sequence of prime numbers.

104. HOLE IN ONE

Answer = 55

Start at the top left of the diagram, and move to the right. Then move down one row and move to the left. Finally move down one row and to the right, making a snakes and ladders pattern. Add together the first two numbers to get the next one along. Repeat this formula while you move around the diagram.

105. MAGIC SQUARE

1	12	8	13
15	6	10	3
14	7	11	2
4	9	5	16

106. MISFITS

A = 71 All the numbers contain a 4

B = 34 All the numbers contain a 7

C = 26 All the numbers contain a 3

D = 19 All the numbers contain a 2

107. BOXING CLEVER

Answer = 82

Multiply each number by 3 and subtract 2 to get the next.

108. MISSING NUMBERS

Answer = 7 and 7

The numbers in each of the segments in the bottom flowers are equal to the sum of the corresponding segments in the connected flowers above.

Left and centre flowers:

1 + 7 = 8

5 + 3 = 8

4 + 2 = 6

6 + 1 = 7

Centre and right flowers:

7 + 1 = 8

3 + 4 = 7

2 + 5 = 7

1 + 3 = 4

109. HONEYCOMB

Answer = 23

All the other numbers are even.

110. HOLE NUMBERS

Answer = 55

Starting in the top left corner and moving clockwise in a spiral pattern towards the centre, add together the previous two numbers to get the next.

111. SUDOKU

2	6	7	4	5	1	8	3	9
3	4	5	9	2	8	6	1	7
9	8	1	6	3	7	2	4	5
4	3	2	1	6	5	9	7	8
6	5	8	7	9	4	1	2	3
1	7	9	2	8	3	4	5	6
8	2	4	5	7	6	3	9	1
5	9	6	3	1	2	7	8	4
7	1	3	8	4	9	5	6	2

112. FIGURE-IT-OUT

Answer = 180

Subtract the number in the third column from the number in the first to get the figure in the middle.

113.SHAPE UP

Answer = 3

Multiply each pair of opposite numbers in each box to get the same answer.

114. HOUSEY HOUSEY

Answer = 42

In each house, add up the numbers around the windows and roof of the house and double the result, putting this number in the doorway.

115. OPTIONAL EXTRAS

Answer = 46

Move down the left hand column, then up the middle, and down the right hand column. Start by adding 2 to the first number, then add 3, 4, 5 etc. all the way around.

116. NUMBER SQUARE

Add together the 3 numbers in each dark shaded square, and then add the number in the lighter shaded square which is closest to the other 3. Their total will always be 15.

117. MINDBENDER

Jack is 52 and Martha is 39.

118. NUMBER WINDOW

Answer = 2

Start with the top left hand square and move clockwise around the others. The sum of the numbers in each square increases by 5 each time, from 10 to 25.

119. GONE MISSING

Answer = 10

In each row, total up the left and right hand numbers and divide this total by 2 to give the value in the central line.

120. NETWORK

Answer: A = 35 and B = 56
Starting at the top left of each grid and moving to the right, top row then bottom row, numbers follow multiples of 6 for the top grid, 7 for grid A and 8 for the grid B.

121. SUDOKU

2	8	4	6	9	5	3	7	1
1	5	6	3	4	7	8	2	9
7	9	3	8	1	2	5	4	6
3	2	5	4	7	1	6	9	8
8	4	7	9	6	3	2	1	5
9	6	1	5	2	8	7	3	4
6	1	2	7	5	4	9	8	3
4	3	9	2	8	6	1	5	7
5	7	8	1	3	9	4	6	2

122. WHEEL SPIN

Answer = 2 0
21 9

Multiply the numbers in matching segments of the top left and top centre circles to get the numbers shown in the bottom left circle. Repeat this for the top right and top centre circles to find the missing numbers.

123. SPACE ODDITY

Oval A = 55 All numbers are multiples of 8
Oval B = 41 All numbers are multiples of 9

124. TAKE AWAY

Answer = 2678
Taking all four digits in the first and last squares in each column, write them down in numerical order in the middle.

125. DOTTY

Answer = 9
Add together the numbers on each line and write the answer in the middle column.

126. ROGUE NUMBER

A = 14 All the rest are multiples of 3

B = 14 All the rest are multiples of 4

C = 16 All the rest are multiples of 6

D = 22 All the rest are multiples of 7

127. MISSING LINK

Answer = 59

Starting at the figure 3, add 1 x 2 to get 5, then 2 x 2 to get 9, 3 x 2 to get 15 and so on.

128. LINE UP

Line B = 12

Line C = 16

Line D = 28

Line E = 18

Line F = 12

Moving along the row, multiply by two then subtract two and continue this sequence.

129. CHANGE IT

Answer = 3

Multiply the outer two numbers to get the third.

130. OPTIONS

Answer = 12

Moving down the first column, up the second and down the third, add three and then two alternately each step.

131. NUMBER SQUARE

Numbers in each row add up to 34.

13	3	2	16
8	10	11	5
12	6	7	9
1	15	14	4

132. SUDOKU

7	2	5	9	8	4	6	3	1
8	4	9	6	1	3	2	7	5
3	1	6	5	7	2	8	9	4
4	8	2	1	9	5	3	6	7
1	9	7	4	3	6	5	2	8
5	6	3	7	2	8	1	4	9
6	7	1	3	5	9	4	8	2
9	3	8	2	4	1	7	5	6
2	5	4	8	6	7	9	1	3

133. RING THE CHANGES

Answer = 18
Add together the two digits shown in the left and right-hand rings and multiply these answers together to get the number in the central ring.

134. WHACKY WEB

Answer = 7
Start with any number from an outer segment of the web, and add it to the number in the inner segment one place clockwise from the original. This sum is always 10.

135. STAR STRUCK

Answer = 6
Add up the outer numbers and divide it by 3 to get the middle numbers.

136. TRIO

Answer = 15
Multiply the top two numbers and divide it by two to get the bottom number.

137. GRID LOCK

Answer: A = 6 and B = 4
Taking each box individually, the bottom number is three less than the top in grid A and four less in grid B.

138. LINES OF THOUGHT

Line B = 11
Line C = 7
Line D = 13
Line E = 10
Line F = 5
Starting on the left and working to the right, alternately add 4 to the first number, then subtract 1.

139. PYRAMID POINTERS

Answer = 82
Add the bottom two numbers and write your answer, in reverse order,at the top of the triangle.

140. TIME OUT

Answer = D
Starting with the watch on the left and moving to the right, the time on each watch increases by 1 hour and 45 minutes.

141. SUDOKU

7	6	4	2	9	3	8	5	1
3	8	5	7	1	4	6	9	2
2	9	1	5	8	6	7	4	3
1	2	3	6	5	8	9	7	4
4	7	6	9	3	1	5	2	8
8	5	9	4	7	2	3	1	6
9	3	8	1	4	7	2	6	5
5	1	2	8	6	9	4	3	7
6	4	7	3	2	5	1	8	9

142. STAR STRUCK

Answer = 5
In each star, add together the top 3 numbers to get a 2 digit answer, and use the bottom two points of the star to display the 2 digits.

143. ODD ONE OUT

Wheel A = 26
It is the only number not containing a 1.
Wheel B = 30
It is the only number not containing a 2.

144. CRAZY CLOCKS
Answer = D
Digits move one place to the left each step.

145. FIGURE-IT-OUT
Answer = 9
If you add up the numbers in any row or column, their total is always 20.

146. SLICED UP
Answer = 7
Multiply together numbers from matching segments of the upper left and right hand circles and put the results in matching segments of the lower circle.

147. DOTTY DOMINOES
Answer = E
The sum of the spots in each column of dominoes is always 16.

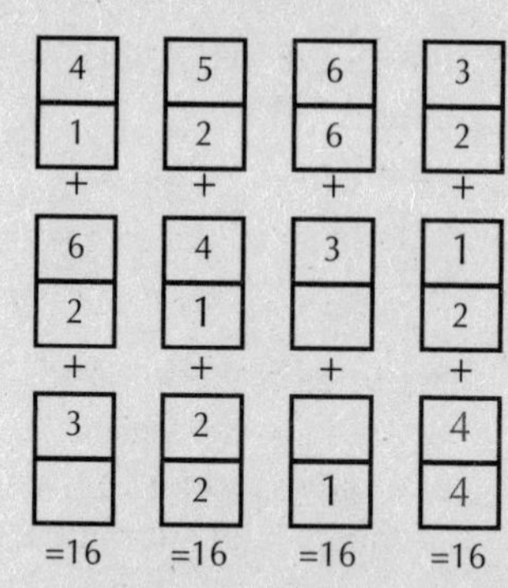

148. PYRAMID POSER
Answer = 24
Multiply the bottom two numbers and double it to get the top number.

149. ALL SQUARE
Add the three outer numbers together and divide by three to get the inner number.

150. DOMINOES
Answer = C
Moving along the rows, the

dots on all four dominoes add up to 18.

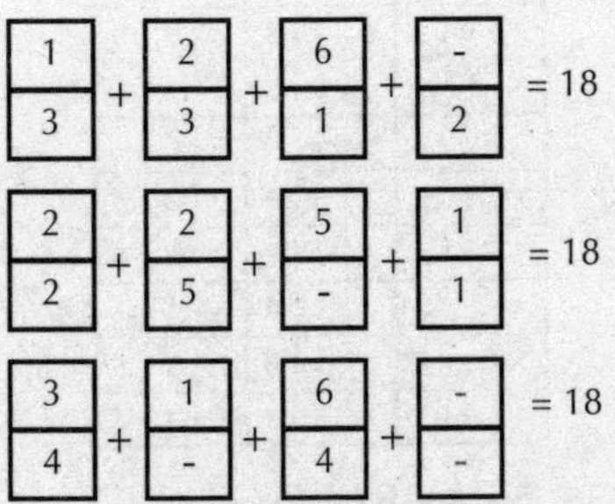

151. CROSS OVER

The middle number in each case is the difference between the numbers on either end of the diagonal lines:

A = 2
B = 3
C = 1

152. TRI-PIE

Answer = 4

Add together the matching segments from the top two pies and transfer the answer to the corresponding segment in the bottom pie.

153. CIRCLES

Answer = 97

Start on the top left, and move clockwise in a spiral towards the centre. Add the first two numbers together to give the next one along. Continue around the rest of the diagram.

154. DIGITAL DISCS

Answer = 8

In each circle, multiply the left and right hand numbers together and add the lower number. The result is always 50.

155. BOXING CLEVER

Answer = 6311

Work through the diagram in columns, top to bottom.

In the left hand column, add 1,100 to each number as you go down. For the central column, add 1,400, and for the right hand column, add 1,700.

156. FOUR SQUARE

Answer = 34

The numbers shown on each point of the diamond are midway between the numbers shown on each point of the square.

157. OUT OF PLACE

Answer = 15

All other numbers in the row are the cube numbers of 1, 2, 3 and 4.

158. SUDOKU

6	8	4	3	1	5	2	7	9
3	7	1	6	2	9	4	5	8
9	5	2	4	7	8	3	1	6
8	2	3	9	5	4	1	6	7
7	4	9	8	6	1	5	2	3
5	1	6	2	3	7	9	8	4
4	6	7	5	9	2	8	3	1
2	3	8	1	4	6	7	9	5
1	9	5	7	8	3	6	4	2

159. NUMBER BOX

Answer = 6

Multiply the first and third numbers in each row and column to get the number in the middle box.

160. MAGIC SQUARE

Answer = 6

The four numbers at the corners of the square when added together equal 20, and the four numbers which make up the diamond when added together also equal 20.

161. WEB WORLD
Answer = 8
When added together each pair of numbers equals 10.

162. ALL STAR
Answer = 16
Starting with the top number and moving clockwise, add 2 to get the next number, then subtract 1, add 2 and then finally subtract 1 again.

163. OUT OF PLACE
Answer = 50
All the other numbers in the cubes are square numbers of 4, 5, 6 and 7.

164. ET CETERA
Answer = 19
Working from left to right, the numbers represent the sequence of Prime Numbers.

165. NUMBER WHEEL
Answer = 2
In each segment of the circle, add the two outer numbers together and subtract the inner number. The result is always 7.

166. SEQUENTIAL
Answer = 63
As you move from left to right, double each number and add 1 to give the next number along.

167. HOLE IN ONE
Answer = 13
Start at the top left of the diagram and move along the row to the right, then down one row and to the left etc in a snakes and ladders pattern. Numbers alternately increase by 3 and then decrease by 1.

168. CIRCLES

Answer = 4

Each line of three numbers going through the centre circle adds up to 12.

169. BOXING CLEVER

Answer = 19

Multiply each number by 2 and then subtract 3 to get the next number.

170. MISSING NUMBERS

Answer = 6 and 6

The numbers in each of the segments in the bottom flowers are equal to double the numbers in the matching segments of the connected flowers above.

Left and centre flowers:

7 + 4 = 11 (22)
2 + 1 = 3 (6)
2 + 1 = 3 (6)
3 + 2 = 5 (10)

Centre and right flowers:

4 + 2 = 6 (12)
3 + 1 = 4 (8)
1 + 4 = 5 (10)
2 + 1 = 3 (6)

171. SUDOKU

1	8	5	7	9	6	3	2	4
7	9	2	4	3	1	6	8	5
3	6	4	2	5	8	7	9	1
2	5	7	3	6	9	1	4	8
4	1	6	8	7	5	9	3	2
9	3	8	1	4	2	5	7	6
5	4	9	6	8	3	2	1	7
8	2	3	5	1	7	4	6	9
6	7	1	9	2	4	8	5	3

172. HONEYCOMB

Answer = 20

All the other numbers are multiples of three.

173. HOLE NUMBERS

Answer = 7

Starting in the top left corner and moving

clockwise in a spiral pattern towards the centre, add 2 for the next number, subtract 1 for the next, add 2, subtract 1 etc.

174. MAGIC SQUARE

10	4	13	7
15	5	12	2
8	14	3	9
1	11	6	16

175. MISFITS

A = 26, B = 26,
C = 12, D = 88
All other numbers are multiples of 4 in Box A, 6 in Box B, 8 in Box C and 13 in Box D.

176. HOUSEY HOUSEY

Answer = 10
Add together the four numbers representing the windows and subtract the number representing the door to get the number shown in the roof.

177. OPTIONAL EXTRAS

Answer = 99
Start at the top of the left hand column, and move down, then to the top of the next column on the right and move down etc. Numbers increase by 5, 7, 9, 11 etc all the way round.

178. NUMBER SQUARE

Add together the 3 digits in each dark grey square, and put this sum in the corner of the light grey square 1/4 turn clockwise from the original square.

179. FIGURE-IT-OUT

Answer = 1109
Add together the numbers in

the first and third columns to get the number in the middle.

180. SUDOKU

8	9	4	6	1	3	2	5	7
5	2	1	4	9	7	3	8	6
7	3	6	5	8	2	9	1	4
1	5	9	8	6	4	7	3	2
3	6	7	1	2	5	4	9	8
2	4	8	3	7	9	5	6	1
9	8	2	7	3	1	6	4	5
4	1	3	2	5	6	8	7	9
6	7	5	9	4	8	1	2	3

181. SHAPE UP

Answer = 5
The sum of the numbers in each square is 24.

182. TAKE AWAY

Answer = 9852
Take all four digits shown in each line and write them in reverse numerical order in the middle.

183. DOTTY

Answer = 7
Add together the numbers in each row and divide it by 2 to get the middle number.

184. ROGUE NUMBER

A = 86, B = 42,
C = 130, D = 110
All the others are square numbers. (2x2 = 4, 3x3 = 9, 4x4 = 16 etc.)

185. MISSING LINK

Answer = 10
Moving from left to right, add 2 for the next number, then subtract 1 for the next and continue this sequence.

186. LINE UP

Line B = 4
Line C = 6
Line D = 4

Line E = 0
Line F = 8
Moving along the rows, subtract 1, add 2, subtract 3, add 4 and then subtract 5.

187. STAR STRUCK
Answer = 88
Add up the outer numbers, add 1 and then write the answer in reverse in the middle.

188. MINDBENDER
Answer = 10 people
Each one shakes hands with 9 other people (90 shakes) with each handshake shared between 2 people (90 ÷ 2 = 45 shakes).

189. SUDOKU

3	8	4	2	9	5	6	7	1
6	5	2	3	1	7	9	8	4
7	9	1	6	4	8	3	5	2
9	1	3	5	8	4	7	2	6
4	7	6	9	2	1	8	3	5
8	2	5	7	3	6	1	4	9
1	6	7	8	5	2	4	9	3
2	4	9	1	7	3	5	6	8
5	3	8	4	6	9	2	1	7

190. NUMBER WINDOW
Answer = 8
In each box, the product of the upper and lower numbers equals the product of the left and right hand numbers.

191. GONE MISSING
Answer = 6
If you add up all the numbers in a row then, from top to bottom, the sums make the sequence 5, 10, 15, 20, 25.

192. NETWORK

Answer A = 18 and B = 24

In each grid, multiply the top left number by 2 to give the lower left number; multiply the top middle number by 3 to give the lower middle number and multiply the top right number by 4 to give the lower right number.

193. CHANGE IT

Answer = 4

Add together the two outer numbers in each segment and add 1 to get the number in the middle.

194. OPTIONS

Answer = 9

Moving down the first column, up the second and down the third, add 4 and then subtract 2 alternately each step.

195. NUMBER SQUARE

Numbers in each row add up to 34.

7	2	9	16
13	12	3	6
4	5	14	11
10	15	8	1

196. WHEEL SPIN

Answer = 14 6
10 2

Start with the top left circle, and move in a W shape around the others, following the line shown. Multiply the numbers in the first circle by 2 and write the results in matching segments of the next circle along. Then subtract 2 from each of these numbers and write the results in matching segments of the next circle. Repeat this pattern, multiplying the numbers by 2, then subtracting 2.

197. SPACE ODDITY
Oval A = 119
All numbers contain the digit 3.
Oval B = 132
All numbers contain 1 digit which is repeated.

198. SUDOKU

6	4	1	5	7	8	2	9	3
3	8	5	9	4	2	7	6	1
2	7	9	1	6	3	5	8	4
8	3	6	2	1	4	9	7	5
9	2	4	7	8	5	3	1	6
1	5	7	3	9	6	8	4	2
5	9	8	4	3	1	6	2	7
7	1	2	6	5	9	4	3	8
4	6	3	8	2	7	1	5	9

199. RING THE CHANGES
Answer = 5
In each row of the diagram, if you subtract the sum of the left and right hand numbers from the central number, the result is always 10.

200. WHACKY WEB
Answer = 22
Start with the central left segment (containing the 3s) and move clockwise around the diagram. The sum of the numbers in the outer and inner segments follow the sequence of multiples of 6, from 6 to 48.

201. STAR STRUCK
Answer = 10
Add up the outer numbers, divide by 2 and then add 3 to get the middle numbers.

202. TRIO

Answer = 41
Multiply the top two numbers and write the answer in reverse at the bottom.

203. GRID LOCK

Answer: A = 9 and B = 25
Square the top numbers in each box to get the bottom number. (3x3 = 9, 5x5 = 25)

204. SUDOKU

8	1	6	5	3	9	2	4	7
3	9	4	6	2	7	1	8	5
2	5	7	4	8	1	6	3	9
4	8	1	9	6	2	7	5	3
9	6	5	8	7	3	4	1	2
7	2	3	1	4	5	8	9	6
6	4	9	2	5	8	3	7	1
1	3	8	7	9	6	5	2	4
5	7	2	3	1	4	9	6	8

205. LINES OF THOUGHT
Line B = 9
Line C = 19
Line D = 5
Line E = 18
Line F = 4
In each row, there are 2 interlinked sequences. Start with the furthest left hand octagon, and move to the right, skipping every other octagon, adding 4 each time. Next, start with the second octagon on the left and move to the right, skipping every other octagon, adding 6 each time.

206. PYRAMID POINTERS
Answer = 25
In each pyramid, multiply the bottom left and right hand numbers together and add the middle number to give the result at the top.

207. TIME OUT
Answer = C
The times shown on the watches would read the same forwards as backwards.

208. STAR STRUCK
Answer = 28
In each star, start at the top and move clockwise around the points of the star. In the left hand star, numbers increase by 1, then 2, then 4 etc. doubling the value each time. Increase the numbers in the middle star by 2, 4, 8 etc. and by 3, 6, 12 etc. in the right hand star.

209. FIGURE-IT-OUT
Answer = 2
If you add up the numbers in each row of the diagram, the total is always 15.

210. SLICED UP

Answer = 6

Subtract numbers in the right hand circle from numbers in matching segments of the left hand circle, putting the results into the lower circle.

211. DOTTY DOMINOES

Answer = D

Work in rows from left to right, top to bottom. Taking consecutive pairs of dominoes, their spot total follows the sequence 5, 6, 7, 8, 9 and 10.

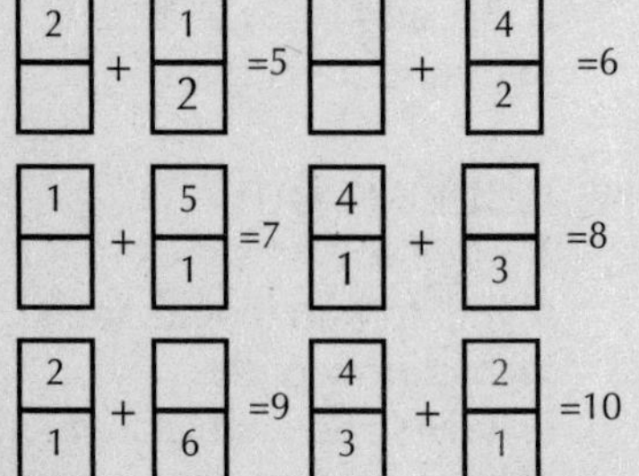

212. ODD ONE OUT

Wheel A = 35

It is the only number not divisible by 9.

Wheel B = 26

It is the only number not divisible by 12.

213. SUDOKU

4	3	1	6	9	2	8	5	7
8	2	6	1	5	7	4	3	9
5	9	7	8	4	3	1	6	2
6	5	2	3	7	8	9	1	4
3	4	8	5	1	9	2	7	6
7	1	9	2	6	4	3	8	5
9	6	4	7	8	1	5	2	3
1	7	3	4	2	5	6	9	8
2	8	5	9	3	6	7	4	1

214. CRAZY CLOCKS

Answer = A

The digits shown on each watch add up to 10 every time.

215. PYRAMID POSER

Answer = 20
Multiply the bottom two numbers together and divide it by 2 to get the top number.
3 x 12 = 36 (18)
4 x 7 = 28 (14)
5 x 8 = 40 (20)

216. ALL SQUARE

Multiply the three outer numbers together to get the number in the middle.

217. DOMINOES

Answer = D
Moving along the lines, add the dots of the first two dominoes together and then subtract the dots from the third to get the answer shown in the last column.

3		2		-		5
1	+	4	-	-	=	5

1		6		1		6
1	+	3	-	-	=	4

-		6		1		5
5	+	5	-	6	=	4

218. CROSS OVER

Multiply the numbers at each end of the diagonal lines to get the middle number.
A = 6
B = 9
C = 18

219. CIRCLES

Answer = 28
Start in the top left corner of the diagram and move in a clockwise spiral towards the centre.
Numbers increase by 3, 4, 5, etc.

220. DIGITAL DISCS

Answer = 14

In each circle, double the right and left hand numbers, then add them together to give the result in the lower segment.

221. BOXING CLEVER

Answer = 20

Treat each 4 digit number as two 2 digit numbers, side by side. In each row, if you add each pair of numbers together, the answer is always the same - 30 for the top row, 35 for the next, then 40, then 45.

222. SUDOKU

5	4	2	9	6	8	1	3	7
1	3	9	2	5	7	8	6	4
6	8	7	4	3	1	2	9	5
2	9	5	1	8	3	4	7	6
4	7	1	6	9	5	3	2	8
8	6	3	7	4	2	9	5	1
7	2	8	5	1	9	6	4	3
3	5	4	8	2	6	7	1	9
9	1	6	3	7	4	5	8	2

223. FOUR SQUARE

Answer = 14

One way of doing this is to start with the 4 on the left and move clockwise. Alternately add 8 to the number, then subtract 3 as you go round.

224. OUT OF PLACE

Answer = 93

All other numbers are multiples of 9.

225. ET CETERA

Answer = 23

Start on the left and move to the right, skipping every other circle, adding 3 each time. Starting with the second circle on the left, and skipping every other circle as before, add 7 each time.

226. TRI-PIE

Answer = 6

Add together the matching segments from the top two pies and transfer the answer to the corresponding segment in the bottom pie.

227. NUMBER BOX

Answer = 14

Multiply together the first and second numbers in each line and then divide it by 2 to get the number in the third box.

228. WEB WORLD

Answer = 2

The numbers in the inner ring match those of the outer ring in the opposite segment.

229. MAGIC SQUARE

Answer = 1

The four numbers at the corners of the square when multiplied together = 24, and the four numbers which make up the diamond when multiplied together = 24.

230. SUDOKU

4	7	2	9	6	5	1	3	8
3	5	1	2	4	8	6	7	9
8	6	9	7	1	3	2	5	4
2	4	7	6	3	1	9	8	5
1	8	6	5	9	4	7	2	3
9	3	5	8	2	7	4	6	1
7	1	3	4	8	6	5	9	2
6	9	4	3	5	2	8	1	7
5	2	8	1	7	9	3	4	6

231. ALL STAR
Answer = 5
Starting with the top number and moving clockwise, double each number and subtract 1 to get the next.

232. CIRCLES
Answer = 19
The middle number is midway between the other two numbers on each line.

233. BOXING CLEVER
Answer = 106
Add three to each number and double it to get the next.

234. NUMBER WHEEL
Answer = 9
Add the outer number of any segment with the inner number from the segment opposite. Their total is always 15.

235. SEQUENTIAL
Answer = 108
As you move to the right, double each number and add 4 to give the next one along.

236. HOLE IN ONE
Answer = 42
Start on the top left of the square and move down. Then right one space and up etc in a snakes and ladders pattern. Numbers increase alternately by 5, then 4.

237. MAGIC SQUARE

25	10	3	6	21
22	12	19	8	4
11	9	13	17	15
2	18	7	14	24
5	16	23	20	1

238. MISFITS

A = 91, B = 49,
C = 95, D = 62
In A and C the second digit in each two-digit number is one higher than the first digit, in B and D they are one lower.

239. HOUSEY HOUSEY

Answer = 5
In each house, the number in the doorway equals the average of the 5 numbers that surround it.

240. OPTIONAL EXTRAS

Answer = 77
Start at the top left corner and move to the right, then down one row and to the left etc in a snakes and ladders pattern. Numbers increase by 2, 4, 6, 8, 10 etc.

241. SUDOKU

6	1	8	4	7	3	2	5	9
9	4	2	1	5	6	8	7	3
7	5	3	2	9	8	1	4	6
3	9	1	6	4	2	5	8	7
2	6	5	7	8	1	3	9	4
8	7	4	5	3	9	6	1	2
1	3	9	8	6	7	4	2	5
5	8	6	9	2	4	7	3	1
4	2	7	3	1	5	9	6	8

242. MISSING NUMBERS

Answer = 9 and 9
The numbers in each of the segments in the bottom flowers are equal to the sum, minus 1, of the corresponding segments in the connected flowers above.
Left and centre flowers:
7 + 3 - 1 = 9
2 + 2 - 1 = 3
3 + 8 - 1 = 10
9 + 1 - 1 = 9

Centre and right flowers:
3 + 4 - 1 = 6
2 + 9 - 1 = 10
8 + 2 - 1 = 9
1 + 6 - 1 = 6

243. HONEYCOMB
Answer = 34
All the other numbers are multiples of 8.

244. HOLE NUMBERS
Answer = 8
Starting in the top left corner and moving clockwise in a spiral pattern towards the centre, add 3 for the next number, subtract 2, and continue this sequence.

245. FIGURE-IT-OUT
Answer = 2594
The three numbers in each row add up to 10,000.

246. SHAPE UP
Answer = 4
Add together the top and bottom numbers. Subtract the right-hand number from the left. The answer is always the same.

247. NUMBER WINDOW
Answer = 4
In each square, multiply the top and bottom numbers together, and the left and right numbers together. The sum of these 2 products is always 20.

248. GONE MISSING
Answer = 10
Add together the numbers in the white circles on each row, divide this answer by 2 and subtract 1 to get the number in the black circle.

249. SUDOKU

2	4	3	6	9	8	7	5	1
6	1	7	5	2	4	9	8	3
8	5	9	7	1	3	6	2	4
1	6	8	3	4	5	2	9	7
9	3	2	1	8	7	5	4	6
5	7	4	9	6	2	1	3	8
3	8	5	2	7	6	4	1	9
4	9	6	8	5	1	3	7	2
7	2	1	4	3	9	8	6	5

250. NETWORK

Answer: A = 11 and B = 17
Working in columns, add the top numbers to the bottom numbers, and add 1 to give the central number.

251. WHEEL SPIN

Answer = 2 11
2 3
Multiply the numbers in matching segments of the top left and top middle circles to get the numbers in the bottom left circle. Repeat this using matching segments of the top right and top middle circles for the bottom right circle.

252. SPACE ODDITY

Oval A = 45
All numbers have a 9 digit in them.
Oval B = 13
All numbers are multiples of 9.

253. TAKE AWAY

Answer = 8131
Reverse the digits shown in the small ovals (left then right) and write the figure in the middle.

254. DOTTY

Answer = 7
Taking the number shown on each side as a whole

number, subtract the right-hand side from the left-hand side. (701 - 694 = 7)

255. ROGUE NUMBER

A = 20, B = 33,
C = 15, D = 39
All the rest are prime numbers. (Numbers that are only divisible by themselves and 1.)

256. MISSING LINK

Answer = 630
Moving from left to right, multiply by 5 for the next number, subtract 4 for the next and continue this sequence.

257. LINE UP

Line B = 3
Line C = 4
Line D = 36
Line E = 5
Line F = 11
Moving along the row, subtract 1, multiply by 2, subtract 3, multiply by 4 and then subtract 5.

258. SUDOKU

9	7	5	8	3	4	6	1	2
1	6	4	9	2	7	8	3	5
3	2	8	6	5	1	7	4	9
7	9	1	4	6	3	5	2	8
5	4	2	1	9	8	3	7	6
6	8	3	2	7	5	1	9	4
4	5	9	3	1	6	2	8	7
8	1	7	5	4	2	9	6	3
2	3	6	7	8	9	4	5	1

259. RING THE CHANGES

Answer = 14
Working in rows, calculate the difference between the left and right hand numbers and double it to give the result in the central ring.

260. WHACKY WEB
Answer = 5
In each slice of the web, multiply the outer segment number by 2 and subtract 3 to give the number in the inner segment.

261. CHANGE IT
Answer = 4
The numbers in each segment add up to 15.

262. OPTIONS
Answer = 17
Moving down the first column, up the second and down the third, double the first number to get the second, then subtract 5 for the third and continue this sequence.

263. NUMBER SQUARE
Numbers in each row add up to 65.

5	2	11	22	25
16	18	9	12	10
23	7	13	19	3
20	14	17	8	6
1	24	15	4	21

264. STAR STRUCK
Answer = 36
Add up the outer numbers and write the answer in reverse in the middle.

265. TRIO
Answer = 71
Multiply the top two numbers, subtract 1 and write the answer in reverse in the bottom segment.

266. GRID LOCK
Answer: A = 14 and B = 11
The numbers in the third boxes in each row and column are the sum of the

digits in the first two boxes.

267. SUDOKU

8	1	6	2	3	7	4	9	5
5	4	2	6	9	8	1	3	7
7	9	3	1	5	4	8	6	2
2	7	9	8	6	3	5	4	1
6	8	5	4	1	9	2	7	3
1	3	4	7	2	5	6	8	9
9	6	7	5	4	1	3	2	8
3	2	1	9	8	6	7	5	4
4	5	8	3	7	2	9	1	6

268. LINES OF THOUGHT

Line B = 10
Line C = 9
Line D = 20
Line E = 6
Line F = 30

Starting on the left of every row and moving to the right, add 4 to the first number, then 5 to the next. Repeat this sequence, alternately adding 4 then 5.

269. PYRAMID POINTERS

Answer = 30

In each pyramid, multiply the lower two numbers together to give the top number, then halve this to give the number in the centre.

270. TIME OUT

Answer = C

Increase all digits by 1 and then move all digits to the left, with the first digit being moved to the far right. For example – 210 becomes 321 after adding 1, changing to 213 when the first digit is moved to the far right.

271. STAR STRUCK

Answer = 6

Multiply the numbers shown on the left-hand side, repeat this for the numbers on the right. The top number is the difference between these two answers.

272. FIGURE-IT-OUT

Answer = 15

Working in columns, add the top number to the middle number and divide this total by 2 to give the lower number.

273. SLICED UP

Answer = 18

Start with the number in

the top left circle, and add 5 to each one to give the results in matching segments of the lower circle. Next, add 6 to each of the numbers in the lower circle to give the results in matching segments of the top right circle.

274. DOTTY DOMINOES

Answer = A

Working in columns, add the spot total of the upper domino to the lower domino, to give the spot total of the central domino.

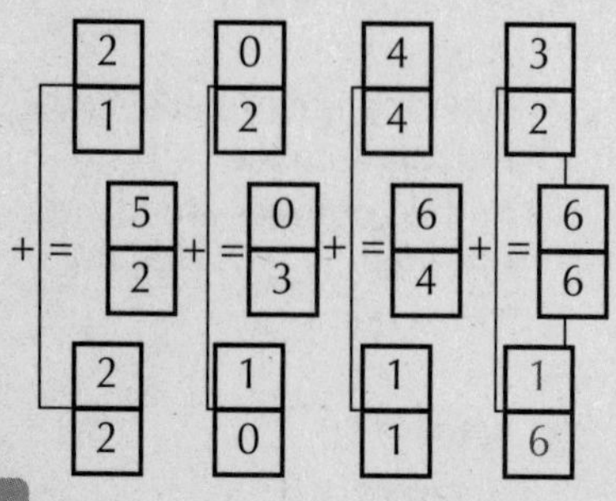

275. CIRCLES

Answer = 49

Start at the top left and move to the right, then down one row and to the left etc. like a snakes and ladders pattern. Add 5 to the first number, then 6, then 7, repeating this sequence as you move around the square.

276. ODD ONE OUT

A = 29, B = 116

All other numbers are square numbers.

277. CRAZY CLOCKS

Answer = B

The digits shown on the minutes side equal double the total of the digits shown on the hour side.

278. PYRAMID POSER

Answer = 10

Add the bottom digits together to get the top number.
2 + 1 + 3 + 7 = 13
1 + 4 + 2 + 3 = 10
1 + 7 + 2 + 0 = 10

279. ALL SQUARE
Multiply the outer three numbers and divide by 2 to get the inner number.

280. SUDOKU

7	8	1	9	6	2	3	4	5
2	4	9	5	1	3	8	7	6
5	6	3	4	7	8	2	9	1
1	3	2	6	8	9	7	5	4
8	7	4	3	5	1	6	2	9
6	9	5	7	2	4	1	8	3
9	1	7	8	4	6	5	3	2
3	2	8	1	9	5	4	6	7
4	5	6	2	3	7	9	1	8

281. DOMINOES
Answer = F
Moving along the lines, the dots on each domino increase by three each step.

-	2	1	6
-	1	5	3
1	2	3	5
-	2	4	5
-	4	4	6
2	1	4	5

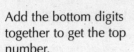

282. CROSS OVER
Multiply the numbers on each end of the diagonal lines and add each answer together to get the middle number.
A = 2, B = 2, C = 31

283. TRI-PIE
Answer = 8
Each pair of opposite numbers equals 10.

284. NUMBER BOX
Answer = 6
Add up the first two numbers in each row and column and then add 1 to get the last number.

285. DIGITAL DISCS
Answer = 12
In each circle, multiply the left and right hand numbers together and divide the result by 3 to give the lower number.

286. BOXING CLEVER
Answer = 6
Work in rows, from top to bottom. If you add up the separate digits in each 4 digit number, you get the same result for each row - in the first row, the total is always 12, for the second it's 13, then 14, then 15 for the bottom row.

287. FOUR SQUARE
Answer = 6
Look at the diagram as 2 intersecting squares, at 45 degrees to each other. The sum of the digits in each square equals 45.

288. OUT OF PLACE
Answer = 36
All other numbers are multiples of 8.

289. ET CETERA
Answer = 44
Start on the left and move to the right. Add the first two numbers together to give the next one, then add 2 to this number to give the one after that. Repeat this sequence all the way along.

290. NUMBER WHEEL
Answer = 6
In each segment, multiply the 2 outer numbers together and divide the result by 2, putting the answer in the inner part of the opposite segment.

291. SEQUENTIAL
Answer = 125
Working from left to right, numbers follow the sequence of cube numbers.

292. SUDOKU

7	2	3	9	6	8	1	5	4
8	1	5	7	2	4	3	6	9
6	4	9	1	3	5	8	7	2
3	6	4	2	7	1	9	8	5
2	7	8	5	4	9	6	3	1
5	9	1	6	8	3	4	2	7
9	3	6	4	5	2	7	1	8
4	8	2	3	1	7	5	9	6
1	5	7	8	9	6	2	4	3

293. WEB WORLD
Answer = 5
The numbers in each of the four opposite segments (inner and outer rings) add up to 20.

294. MAGIC SQUARE
Answer = 6
Multiply the four numbers in the square to get the same answer as when you multiply the four numbers in the diamond. This gives the figure in the middle.

295. ALL STAR
Answer = 18
Starting with the top number and moving anti-clockwise, double each number and subtract 2 to get the next number.

296. CIRCLES
Answer = 4
Add together the numbers

on the end of each line and double it to get the middle number in the grid.

297. BOXING CLEVER

Answer = 36
The numbers will be the first five square numbers. (2x2 = 4, 3x3 = 9, 4x4 = 16, 5x5 = 25 and 6x6 = 36)

298. MISSING NUMBERS

Answer = 7 and 7
The numbers in each of the segments in the bottom flowers are equal to half the sum of the matching segments in the connected flowers above.
Left and centre flowers:
7 + 9 = 16 (8)
4 + 6 = 10 (5)
2 + 10 = 12 (6)
9 + 7 = 16 (8)
Centre and right flowers:
9 + 5 = 14 (7)
6 + 6 = 12 (6)
10 + 4 = 14 (7)
7 + 3 = 10 (5)

299. HONEYCOMB

Answer = 54
The digits shown in the other numbers always add up to 10.

300. HOLE IN ONE

Answer = 259
Moving in a spiral pattern, anti-clockwise, double each number and subtract 3 each step.

301. MAGIC SQUARE

11	18	25	2	9
10	12	19	21	3
4	6	13	20	22
23	5	7	14	16
17	24	1	8	15

302. MISFITS

A = 33, B = 23,
C = 16, D = 34
In each square all digits, when added together, equal 8.

303. HOLE NUMBERS

Answer = 14
Starting in the top left corner and moving clockwise in a spiral pattern towards the centre, add 9, subtract 8, add 7, subtract 6, etc.

304. FIGURE-IT-OUT

Answer = 8068
Add together the numbers in the first and third columns and write the answer in reverse in the middle column.

305. SHAPE UP

Answer = 5
Multiply the top and bottom numbers and write the answer as single digits on the left and right.

306. SUDOKU

8	1	5	4	6	2	9	7	3
4	6	2	9	7	3	1	8	5
7	3	9	1	5	8	4	2	6
6	9	3	7	1	4	2	5	8
5	2	4	8	3	9	6	1	7
1	8	7	6	2	5	3	9	4
3	7	1	5	9	6	8	4	2
9	4	6	2	8	7	5	3	1
2	5	8	3	4	1	7	6	9

307. TAKE AWAY

Answer = 7647
Taking all four digits shown in the left and right rectangles write this figure down in reverse in the middle.

308. DOTTY

Answer = 9
The figure in the middle

column is the same as the highest number in each row.

309. HOUSEY HOUSEY

Answer = 13

In each house, start at the roof and work clockwise around the windows, Add the doorway number to the first number to give the next one along. Continue like this, but subtracting 1 from the doorway number each time.

310. OPTIONAL EXTRAS

Answer = 158

Start on the top left and move down, then right one place and up, then right one place and down again, in a snakes and ladders pattern. Add the first 2 numbers together, and subtract 1 to give the next number along.

311. NUMBER SQUARE

Add together the 3 numbers in each box, then put this sum in the corner of the middle box, a half turn clockwise from the original box.

312. MINDBENDER

Answer = Paul, Peter and Andrew should all give John 1 sweet each.

Calculate it like so - John is owed 4 sweets, but owes 1 himself, leaving him 3 sweets short. Paul owes 2 sweets, but is also owed 1 by John, making a total of 1 sweet owed. Follow the same pattern, to reveal Peter and Andrew also owe 1 sweet each. They each give the 1 sweet they owe to John, who is owed 3 sweets.

313. NUMBER WINDOW

Answer = 6

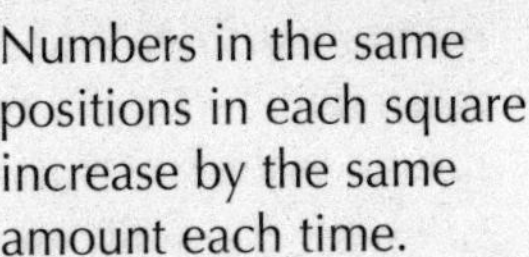

Numbers in the same positions in each square increase by the same amount each time.

314. GONE MISSING

Answer = 11
Work through the diagram in rows, from top to bottom, left to right. In the first row, numbers increase by 3 as you move to the right. In the second row, numbers increase by 4 etc. until in the final row numbers increase by 7.

315. SUDOKU

2	5	8	1	4	6	9	7	3
7	6	1	9	2	3	4	8	5
9	4	3	8	7	5	2	1	6
1	9	4	7	6	8	5	3	2
5	7	2	3	9	4	1	6	8
8	3	6	2	5	1	7	4	9
6	1	7	5	3	2	8	9	4
3	2	9	4	8	7	6	5	1
4	8	5	6	1	9	3	2	7

316. ROGUE NUMBER

A = 720, B = 864,
C = 324, D = 1020
All other numbers are cube numbers (2x2x2 = 8, 3x3x3 = 27 etc.)

317. MISSING LINK

Answer = 165
Moving from left to right, multiply by 5 for the next number, then subtract 7 for the next and continue this sequence.

318. LINE UP

Line A = 28
Line B = 12
Line C = 8
Line D = 24
Line E = 54
Line F = 73
Moving along the rows, divide by 2, add 4, multiply by 3, add 7 and subtract 3.

319. CHANGE IT

Answer = 4

The total of the numbers in each segment increases by 1 moving clockwise around the circle.

320. NETWORK

Answer A = 5 and B = 6

In each grid, working in rows, the sum of the digits in the top row equals 10, the sum of the digits in the second row equals 15 and the sum of the digits in the bottom row equals 20.

321. WHEEL SPIN

Answer = 15 17
20 16

Start with the left hand circle and move along the lines, in a W shape. Add 2 to the numbers in the first circle, putting the results in matching segments of the next circle. Then add 3 to these numbers, putting the results in the next circle. Continue this pattern, adding 4 and then 5.

322. SPACE ODDITY

Oval A = 72

All numbers are square numbers.

Oval B = 109

All numbers are cube numbers.

Puzzle It Out!

Use these handy pages to work out the trickiest puzzles.

Puzzle It Out!

Use these handy pages to work out the trickiest puzzles.

Puzzle It Out!

Use these handy pages to work out the trickiest puzzles.

Puzzle It Out!

Use these handy pages to work out the trickiest puzzles.

Puzzle It Out!

Use these handy pages to work out the trickiest puzzles.

Puzzle It Out!

Use these handy pages to work out the trickiest puzzles.